Still Life

Still Life

Capturing that special moment in time.

By
Jennifer P. Lumley

iUniverse, Inc.
New York   Bloomington

STILL LIFE
Capturing that special moment in time by richly depicting realistic perspectives.

iUniverse books may be ordered through booksellers or by contacting:

iUniverse
1663 Liberty Drive
Bloomington, IN 47403
www.iuniverse.com
1-800-Authors (1-800-288-4677)

ISBN: 978-1-4502-4246-2 (sc)
ISBN: 978-1-4502-4247-9 (ebook)

Printed in the United States of America

iUniverse rev. date: 9/15/2010

FOREWORD

Still Life is the second instalment in the series of rich and exciting poetry collections authored by Jennifer Lumley. This culminates a journey that has spanned some thirty years and marks the firm establishment of Ms. Lumley as a seasoned author. I am fortunate to have witnessed her transition from her first book "Mind Shaper" to the new world of "Still Life" and I am ecstatic to have participated in the continuous effort of attempting to better the previous masterpiece. Success is just reward for a job well done and the extent to which the attempt has been successful is in the eyes and hearts of the readers. Mind Shaper has captivated a solid fan base and Still Life can only expand it. Whatever happens, it is still life.

Maurice Fletcher
Principal Lecturer,
Mechanical & Industrial Engineer.

EPIGRAPH

"The foundation of all foundations and the pillar of all wisdom is to know that there is a God who brought into being all existence. All the beings of the heavens, and the earth, and what is between them came into existence only from the truth of God's being."

Moses Maimonides
[aka Moshe ben Maimon - Jewish philosopher]

"Who is this that darkeneth counsel by words without knowledge? Gird up now thy loins like a man; for I will demand of thee, and answer thou me. Where wast thou when I laid the foundations of the earth? declare, if thou hast understanding. Who hath laid the measures thereof, if thou knowest? or who hath stretched the line upon it? Whereupon are the foundations thereof fastened? or who laid the corner stone thereof; When the morning stars sang together, and all the sons of God shouted for joy? Or who shut up the sea with doors, when it brake forth, as if it had issued out of the womb?"

Job 38:2-8

'Capturing that special moment in time by richly depicting realistic perspectives. Irrespective of that personal experience, it is STILL LIFE.'

PREFACE

In creating **STILL LIFE**, I have embraced the truth and dignity we owe to ourselves and to our environment. I have deliberately included invaluable pieces that create a sense of nostalgia and some other pieces that honor beauty, love, spirituality and culture.

Having published my previous work, **MIND SHAPER,** and having had the warm experiences that came as each copy was sold, there was no option but to continue with the same or more tenacity for **STILL LIFE**, that made **MIND SHAPER** such a success. Stress, which is sometimes a necessary element for growth and focus, when taken positively, is what I experienced after having written once, and it has now forced me to continue to produce emphatically prominent pieces.

I was, and still am, enthused by the growing demand for my work, my performances and my presence at delightfully unexpected venues.

I owe it to myself and to my readers to remain determined to be enlightened, as I am reminded in **Romans 12:2[AMP]** *"Do not be conformed to this world, but be transformed by the entire renewal of your mind…"*

About The Author

A native of Jamaica, Jennifer Lumley migrated to the US some thirty years ago and settled in Westchester County, New York. Having graduated from Marymount College in Tarrytown, NY, where she earned a Bachelor's degree in Business Administration/ Finance, Lumley continued in her banking career, earned her New York State Life Accident and Health Insurance Licence, became a Licensed Financial Specialist/Advisor and an Authorized Lender throughout the continental United States, yet she has always found quiet, personal joy and satisfaction in writing and delighted many when she published her first book of poetry, MIND SHAPER.

Ms. Lumley has hosted workshops and given personal guidance on "How to Deliver an Oral Presentation", Dollars and ene, "Saving for your Retirement", "Education & College Planning" and a host of others, which allowed her to better understand some of the financial challenges facing the community at large, especially new immigrants but in particular the Caribbean Diaspora. Ms. Lumley's clients have all been better able to make informed decisions regarding their finances. Jennifer Lumley opted out of the corporate world and is now an internationally published author concentrating her energies as a Creative/Special Events Writing Instructor, making public appearances as a Cultural Poet/ Mistress of Ceremonies and of course augmenting of her craft using different genres of writing.

She takes with her, more of the same tenacity, passion, pride, patience and understanding that she had in the corporate world, to her readers. Salient to everything else is the fact that her books are 'home grown' designed to inspire, awaken and enlighten the senses and give children and adults alike, the impetus to strive to do the same or better. Lumley's book is inclusive of, but not limited to, history, Japanese haikus, meditation, laughter and 'eye-openers'. She has successfully set out to create an internationally recognized literary work of fine art, worthy of being a good supplement to literature, film, the English language and creative writing. Sections of her work give a good glimpse of what other cultures do in literature and in life, thus, mention of words or phrases in Asante (Ghana), English, French, German, Italian, Japanese, Latin, Polish, Spanish, Twi, (Ghana) and of course the JAMAICAN dialect.

The Author believes that standard English was never enough to effectively deliver the hosts of thoughts and ideas she has had on her mind, such as the socio-economic and politically charged atmosphere, the feisty market people who were entrepreneurial in their own way, the mellow men in rum bars who drank white rum and played skittle on Friday evenings, those ladies who quarrelled in tenement yards, and 'pickney' who fought over unfair marble games. Jennifer Lumley still finds the Jamaican language, also called patois, to be so rich, spicy and flavourful, that she always wondered why it wasn't used by more people. By including it in her work, as well as in her cultural performances, book signings and radio presentations, Lumley has captured a much wider audience, clamouring in appreciation, for more on each occasion.

Jennifer Lumley has been described as "a modern day Louise Bennett in America," but the author simply wants our sweet-sweet culture to follow us wherever we decide to take up residence and raise wholesome children. By recounting stories, the richness of the culture will not be "watered down" or lost. Lumley finds no substitute for the parlance that's called 'JAMAICAN'.

ALSO BY JENNIFER LUMLEY

Mind Shaper

Faith's Pivotal Role in Altered Cultures

Dedication

My God and King, my Saviour dear,
Who is forever with me everywhere.

My devoted Mother, Amy. Mamie, as she is more affectionately known
has shown unmatched support and has made a world of difference
in my life. She is the model of an economically self reliant mother,
who still places great importance on always doing your best.
My Mother still believes.

VISION: Determined to be enlightened.

MISSION STATEMENT: Consciously determined to orderly arrange life choices necessary to be more enlightened and to perform above expectations.

Acknowledgements

Ralston "Rex" Nettleford, a fellow Montegonian, a professor, a writer and orator extra-ordinaire, who became the celebrated Caribbean Cultural Ambassador to preserve the cultural life of Jamaica through the dance medium and openly praising persons like "Miss Lou," who brought poetry and song, when many others either frowned upon it or didn't think it important. The National Dance Theatre Company, (Jamaica), and the University of the West Indies will only have to build from his vision, in an attempt to fill the icon-shaped void that is now left.
I am privileged to be standing on the shoulders of persons such as these, who carved a way for my cultural work to be so readily accepted. THANK YOU Mr. Nettleford!

****

My audience, supporters, well-wishers and friends that have invited me to share in their various enterprises and referred me over and over again to fit the needs of additional audiences. In particular, Barbara M. Simpson, (deceased) who caused me to pay keener attention to my work.

****

Lestah Kool from CaribBlast who conducted the My-Space interview. Series #13. Who said thirteen was not a lucky number?

****

The friends and family members who continue to believe in shaping minds...positively!

****

My biggest critic, Maurice G. Fletcher, strikes again. Maurice is also responsible for relieving my angst and providing all of the graphics. He constantly reminds me of how good a work I have already done and is a true source of encouragement.

Table of Contents

Section 1)
STILL LIFE

I AM

I am just who I am
And I don't have a plan,
Nor does a plan have me,
To be anyone but whom I am;
Otherwise I wouldn't be me!

DIAMOND AND I

Diamond and I
Alone; and she purrs,
While she sprawls.
Position of total trust;
Vulnerable.

ON MY TERMS

I don't want a funeral;
Just throw my corpse to sea;
Let the fish tear me apart,
Like you have all done to me.

LADY BLUE

Lady Blue" is a delightful painting of a violin done by artist Paul Blackwood. There is more to it than meets the eye.

She sings no song but knows them all,
She sits down short but stands up tall.
Musicians know her from all over town;
The touch of a bow will remove any frown.

She becomes that happy-go-lucky girl;
A lady to make you dance with a twirl,
Or tap your feet, listening to jazz with a beat.
All genres of music; Baroque, classical and folk heat.

The sound post conducts vibrations in front and back;
The bridge is essential so sound quality never lacks.
The scroll decorates the top of this hand-carved violin;
The chin-rest frees up the hand because it's for the **chin.**

The peg box and 'F' holes and nut and the tailpiece,
Are all so important in playing a masterpiece;
And all four strings that are tuned a fifth apart,
Mark the beginning of this truly, fine art.

Lady Blue has cousins and when they all get together,
You will dance all night because you're light as a feather.
Cousin Viola, and Cello and Double Bass and Fiddle,
Play tremolo, sul ponticello and pizzicato like a riddle.

Violinists: Bach, Bartok, Beethoven, Brahms,
Debussy, Mendelssohn, Mozart, Schuman,
Schubert, Scheonberg, Stravinsky, Tchaikovsky.
I wonder if they ever used my Stradivari?

YOU HAVE TO WRITE

You have to write when it is right;
You have to write when it is so;
You have to write the thoughts of others.
Write well and then be on the go.

You have to write when others ask you;
You have to write even when they don't;
You have to write for brides and babies;
Write for the corpse six feet below.

You have to write for anniversaries;
You also have to write for birthdays;
You have to write for many journals;
Write bios, speeches and some plays.

You have to write when it really matters;
You have to write when it really counts;
You have to write straight from your heart.
Write and be happy and let it amount.

You have to write and not be pedantic
You have to write and then muse;
You have to write and be ecstatic;
Write and show some fortitude.

You have to write about Mother Nature,
You have to write for the lonely heart,
You have to write on how to cogitate.
Write of new love about to start!

BETWIXT OR BETWEEN

Is there really a difference,
between 'betwixt' and 'between'?
A line of demarcation can't be drawn
The difference can hardly be seen.
Well do I know that they are both
Adverbs and prepositions.
My Concise Oxford Dictionary says so
And to that I have no opposition.

'Between' to me represents
The space separating two objects,
Or an indication of a relationship,
Involving two or more subjects.
'Betwixt' is more like 'intervals'
And I dare say it's more archaic.
A pause, a gap, a break or such,
Something quite like theatrics.

Now with the studies that have been done,
Do we now know what's right?
'Between whom?' or 'betwixt what?'
The subject deserves some light.
Well, while you are doing research,
A cup of tea for you I'll fix;
I'll go to bed and lay think
If I'm 'between' my sheets or 'betwixt'!

Jennifer P. Lumley

GRANDMOTHER'S PRAYER

You enter and she looks at you from far across the room.
What did you do with life today? Work toward your doom?
Or did you smile and bring a cheer in your action and your deeds?
And did you call that sick someone and plant some worthwhile seeds?

She speaks no word but loudly heard it echoes in your head.
You know she knows and well she knows all that is unsaid.
Without reply you walk on by, on other days you'll just sit
In front of her because you know that you will never quit.

Notice her extraordinary details, with book-matched, olive, ash burl.
Graced is her unique swan neck pediment; her beauty does unfurl.
Canted, intricately carved columns, frame the doors of bevelled glass;
The Hampton cherry finish, the polished numerals of raised brass.

And she stands firm with weights all three and pendulum asway;
Carved panels of finest quality, on the door to her entry way.
Vintage umber construction and carved pedestals with classic lines;
Old world elegance of wealth and fame embellished in her designs.

The hypnotic, cast centre pendulum, mirrors the dial and weights;
A tick-tock here and a tick-tock there will make you think you're late.
Up above and down below, flourishes the floral, framing overlays;
Continuous addition to details of the multi-tiered, wrap-around base.

You must hand-crank this lady to hear her triple chime;
Her most famous is the Westminster, associated with Big Ben's time.
The House of Parliament also had it, as did St. Mary's church,
Adjustable levelers under each corner, provide a stable perch.

A Howard Miller Presidential collection boasts its moon phase hemisphere
An heirloom with a reverent melody and a sweet and beautiful prayer
"Lord through this hour, Be thou our guide
So, by Thy power, No foot shall slide"
[Sung]

SIDE FX

My doctor is extremely thorough
For all the years I've known;
He'll ask a question twice to be sure,
Even though you're mature and grown.

On my most recent visit
I shared a little bit of concern,
Two weeks before I didn't rest,
I constantly tossed and turned.

So my doctor made a recommendation
And he told me not to fret;
But the description of his plan for me
Made my **'you-know-what'** get wet.

What he prescribed for sleepless nights,
He said had a few side effects.
You'll certainly understand my fright
And why I would start to fret.

He said that I shouldn't drive,
Or operate any kind of machinery;
And get at least eight hours of rest,
Otherwise I could become hallucinatory.

Sleep-walking, abnormal eating habits,
Depression and aggressive behaviour,
Allergic reactions, shortness of breath,
Throat swelling; my good Lord and Saviour!

He continued to describe these few,
These few side effects mentioned earlier;
The drowsiness, dizziness and headaches,
Memory loss, suicide and diarrhea.

I turned my thoughts quickly again,
To that night when I tossed and turned,
And recalled that on that summer day,
I had got a little sunburn.

So up I got and quickly thanked
My wonderful doctor dear;
I have not had a restlessness night
Since I got that awful scare!!!

LATE NIGHT

Late night phone call;
Loneliness ends;
Discomfort eased;
Warm thoughts of
Love, showers.

ROSE PETAL

Rose petal skin,
Gently touched,
Responds; welcomes
Sweet embrace and
Soothing caresses.

SPEECH AND THOUGHT

Sometimes you are so quiet,
Even though you are speaking aloud.
Your thoughts are sincere and simple
Especially in a crowd.

LAKERA WEST

In any test,
Put against the rest,
You're the best;
And yes,
You hold your chest
Up high and 'fess
It was a mess,
But simply jest,
You had to start
To massage and caress
The words in your heart.
Nothing less,
No pest in a nest,
Could stop your quest;
Oh no, no…Lakera West.

SHERNETTE AT FIFTY

Shernette is her real first name,
Hall was family acquired;
Energetic and fiercely protective
Rose above all; never tired.
Nice and pleasant but always real,
Enthusiastic and never bored
Thinking constantly of her survival;
Thanking God for her little brood.
Electrifying, a real pal; now fifty and phenom-
enal!!!

Congratulations, Happy Birthday and may God
ever bless you.

JOE GIBSON'S DEATH

Please don't die Joe Gibson's death,
Especially on a Friday night.
Joe died a really awful death.
From his body, his soul took flight.

All because he worked so hard
For a girl he truly loved.
She carried their babe so carefully;
Their precious gift from God above.

Joe would have been a really great dad
But never saw his baby girl.
Like me, she'll only have a mother;
No Father to defend her in this world.

Joe had a dream there in his car,
He never did awaken;
Behind the steering wheel he sat;
Now he is safe in heaven.

The day I got news of Joe's death,
They wouldn't let me see him.
My treasured friend and confidante,
From earth they finally freed him.

So if on a Friday night you tire,
Don't ever brave that trip.
Rest some place then start again,
You will be far more equipped.

I'M A MOTHER

I'm a mother.
Not just bearing children,
But also rearing children.
Knowing each personality;
Teaching class and dignity;
Learning new adventures
When the homework comes.
Setting good example,
Shining like a beacon of light,
Helping to carve their future bright,
For soon they will be grown,
But still I will be known,
As their Mother!

DECEPTIVE DISPOSITION

Those striking little politicians,
Who go around seeking votes;
Promising to change the world,
By taking notes and oaths.

Smiling with babies and old ladies,
Climbing the ladder another rung;
Appearing in places they'll never revisit;
Singing songs that were already sung.

What if they should be examined
And seen dishonest to the very core?
How come the public simply votes,
Without ever really being sure?

Has it become a prerequisite,
To be a thief or an extortionist?
A willful liar in or out of court?
A bump, a sore with puss or a cyst?

Society should not be so infested,
With behaviours so patronizing;
And chaos, and madness and mayhem.
Frightening and antagonizing!

TONGUE TWISTERS

Purple people pet the panda,
Panda pondered, wept in wonder;
Preacher prayed a pensive prayer,
Now peering at a purple panda.

****

Betty's bigger, better book,
Brought big brother's friends to look,
Blah and boring was the beaver,
But belching bison made them leave her.

****

Cute and cuddly, caring,
Kind and calm caressing,
Courageous kisses caring,
Criss-cross causes crackling.

A CARING HEART

It had to be appropriately said,
It had to be totally sincere;
It had to get your absolute attention,
It made my eye drop a tear.

For every single life you've touched,
And every single organization,
That has been a beneficiary of your love,
There is great appreciation.

Your intellect has helped you to determine
How to handle each situation;
But together with visceral judgement,
You possess a rare combination.

There's no razzamatazz that follows you
Or any anthemic parade;
For you will listen with your ear and heart;
To you, there is no charade.

As I have seen you through the years,
Knowing only some of what you do,
My thoughts can't help but wonder,
When you need help, who do you turn to?

FAITH IN FINANCIAL SPECIALISTS

Two Positive Forms of Identification,
Must first of all be obtained;
A call to *Chexsystems* must be made;
This shows that you've been properly trained.

You've been trained to sell bank products;
Insurance, Investments and Securities.
You must also do a *Credit Check*,
To make sure you cover all bases.

As a Financial Specialist you must know,
Almost everything in the whole world.
Your employer expects you to do your best
Never expecting you to bend the rule.

Here are some other things you must know,
Once you've decided to enter this field;
That many changes are expected to take place,
And for the changes you notice, take heed.

Let's talk about *Checking and Savings Accounts,*
Certificate of Deposits and Money Market;
Christmas Clubs and Overdraft Protection,
H.E. Loan or Home Equity Lines of Credit.

The Traditional or the Roth IRA
Are types of *Individual Retirement Accounts.*
College Five Twenty Nine, Age of Majority;
Transfer assets from Guardian and Custodial plans.

You must be versed in *Debt-to-Income Ratio*;
Recommend *Direct Deposits* and *Mutual Funds.*
Rule of Seventy Two, shows how money doubles.
Then you have *Foreign Currency, Stocks and Bonds.*

Deposits, Withdrawals, Wire Transfers and such,
Deeds, Trusts, Death Certificate and Wills;
Levies, Garnishments and Safe Deposits
And knowing how to identify *Counterfeit Bills*!

You must know all these things and more.
The list is extensive; it's still quite long
Let's continue now, for it feels like
Out of this we could make a song.

Money orders, Drafts and Cashiers' Checks,
Business Plans and Corporate Resolutions;
Credit and Debit Cards and PIN Numbers,
Dollar Cost Averaging, sometimes the best solution.

Power of Attorney, Check Kiting and Address Changes,
Bankruptcies, Check-printing companies;
401K, 403B, 501c)3 and ATMs
And be able to identify *Delinquencies.*

Letters of Testamentary, Letters of Credit and Partnerships,
Minimum Balances required to avoid unnecessary fees;
Knowledge of *APR: Average Percent Rate,*
As opposed to *APY: the Average Percentage Yield.*

Fixed Annuities and Variable Annuities,
The Terms and Conditions that apply;
Merchant Services and Funds Availability Schedule;
Excellent *Customer Service* in extra supply.

Ten Ninety Nine, Non-Profit Organizations
SIPC, FDIC and P.O.D.
Pension, Social Security and Disability
Joint Ownership and T.O.D.

Online Banking, Telephone Transfer and Bill Pay,
Routing Numbers, Electronic Funds Transfer;
The Privacy Act, The Patriotic Act
And Full Account Disclosure.

Be careful with the '*Do Not Call' Policy,*
Watch for *stale dated* and *post dated checks*;
Abandoned Property and Dormant Accounts;
Stop Payments to be put into effect.

Customer Appreciation Day is a treat;
Monthly or Quarterly Statements, an option.
Market Fluctuations you can expect;
Disclose that always in your *Customer Relations.*

Good Faith Estimates, reading the *Ibbotson Chart,*
Being an *Authorized Signer or Notary Public;*
Having the *New York State LAH Insurance License*
Makes you fully equipped and you tick!

This is just some of what you have to know
Once licensed with your *Series 6 and 63;*
Special care should then be taken then
Not to lose, your license, your character or integrity.

Decorative plaques, prizes and recognition
With hard work, you'll get a great deal of;
It's finally paid off after you became a hermit
Studying for months, but now you can laugh.

Be kind to your Financial Specialist
As she advises and helps you to know;
She has not made off with your money;
Continuing Ed classes will help her to grow.

BREATH OF DEATH

Deep thoughts and wonderment run wild,
For the new mother that just gave birth;
Watching as the building came crashing down;
In double pain she lost all her mirth.

An infant new; pure and innocent;
No chance given to breathe or to sin,
Still attached by the throbbing umbilical cord;
Underneath the rubble rested its chin.

The injured doctor's attempts to shift the weight
Of the bricks, that on his shoulder lay,
Made him appear like a little Atlas, in pain;
His first breath was his last on his BIRTH day.

I wonder who was taking a shower,
Or who was out drinking fine wine,
Or who may have been at the church's altar,
Or waiting to buy tickets on a line?

Or teaching children some new lesson,
Or riding a bicycle while whistling;
Or in a gypsy cab heading home;
Or to the day's news just listening?

Picture all the people in a bustle,
At hotels, libraries, restaurants and embassies,
With highest hopes and plans and dreams;
And schedules to fulfill some fantasies.

The pain, the fear, the horrifying sights;
The agony of losing your only brother.
Groan to your God like an injured beast,
"How can I give birth and not be a mother?" Still, life goes on!

TOLERANCE

You don't set out to be unkind,
You certainly don't want to be rude,
But there are some folks who just won't quit;
They know nothing but how to be crude.

And in an attempt to separate yourself
From the company you do not desire;
Somehow, you always bump right back
Into the same old mire.

It seems a trench left open somewhere,
Spewed out some ugly, unwelcome stuff.
These folks tried to copy and mimic that behavior,
That society's got more than enough of.

In order to even try to accommodate
Any conversation on their level,
You mustn't get low and crawl on your belly;
And get mixed up with the filth and the devil.

Keep your thoughts constantly clean.
Don't think for a moment you shan't.
Take the high road; rise above unclean things.
Let no one tell you, that you can't.

The characteristic trait that you must possess,
Is sincere, quantitative compassion,
In understanding the source of their perception,
Then you can actually love that someone.

Section 2)
MATTERS OF THE HEART

QUIETLY, MY LOVE

Between the sheets and in darkness,
The statements are softly spoken.
Hugs and kisses while all alone;
Quietly, my Love gives a token.

A token of the love deeply kept,
In a place almost unknown,
Except for the very fortunate;
Quietly, my Love hath shown.

To have hands held, while walking,
Is so uncommon to some lovers;
A gentle smile when we're talking;
Quietly, my Love, it's treasured.

Music of the heart and soul,
We share so much we're blessed.
And the rhythm of the body;
Quietly, my Love; you're the best.

For all the things you do not say,
Behind the scenes you'll just do,
Actions without noise shout loudly;
Quietly, my Love; I love you.

ALMOST THERE

Almost there,
Almost bare-footed in the park;
Almost there,
Almost shared myself in the dark;
Almost there,
Almost cared to give you my love;
Almost there,
Almost dared but thank heavens above.
Almost there,
Almost feared that now I was lost;
Almost there,
Almost scared that there was a cost;
Almost there,
Almost merely satisfied;
Almost there,
Almost where I got gratified;
Almost there,
Almost gear-shifting out of that place;
Almost there,
Almost a year and an unhappy face;
Almost there,
Almost peer-pressured with new habits;
Almost there,
Almost aware, that I also can have it.
Almost there,
Almost sincere, without a disguise;
Almost there,
Almost there, anywhere, just add some spice.
Almost there,
Almost compromised, not good enough;
Almost there,
NO ALMOST, MEASURE UP OR STEP DOWN, TOO
TOUGH!

CHESTNUT BROWNS

And I looked deeply in those eyes and I knew from the very start,
Those chestnut browns cared from within, mind, soul and heart;
And I had that sweet sensation that warmed me through and through;
A feeling that repeated to me, "I truly do love you".
My love for you does gently glow, with warmth that never burns;
My love for you is constant and from you will never turn.
My love and yours together, will make the darkness bright;
Will bring anthemic cheers and happiness and wonderful delight.

I love you oh so freely, as a butterfly in a splendent field;
As a bee upon a flower, this love thrall is just surreal.
Your love for me is natural and fresh as morning dew,
That touches my rose-petal skin as it whispers "I love you."
There is so much love within our world, gentle as a baby's smile;
The extra-galactic nebula reflects that love from across the miles.
Our love is like the water, from which you quench a dry thirst;
An ocean of endless, blanket tides, from which the waves do burst.

A mountain top on which to climb and view the entire world,
As gentle winds brush our cheeks and cause our toes to curl.
The razzamatazz of this true love, like marzipan rich with flavour,
The almond condiment so rich and sweet, you appreciate and savour.
Is it so strange we never said but knew, that we had fallen in love?
Or stranger still, that we thanked God from heaven up above?
And neither knew the other's act, but we knew that love was in us;
Never mind the distance or the years, we both have God to trust.

Jennifer P. Lumley

CAROUSEL TWELVE

As I went to claim my luggage
Over by carousel number twelve,
I reached for my brown suitcases
And there I got some help.

A most pleasant and strong Latino;
Reached for both pieces together
And stroked the pink name tags hanging,
Between my cases of softest leather.

Carousel twelve was interesting.
I took a spin or two around,
And rode with my new Latino friend
And my brand-name luggage brown.

My plane trip was exciting;
Sat next to a bambino;
More exciting was the language I learned,
When I landed with a Latino.

NEW FEELINGS

New feelings came across my heart,
When I heard your voice today.
Feelings resembling the ones we had;
Those feelings that you didn't say.

New feelings started to dash up and down,
Then gripped my heart really tight;
Feelings I have felt long before
And made my body feel oh so right.

New feelings came along once more,
Smiles lighter than a feather;
Right feelings in my heart were sure,
That's the reason we're together.

New feelings of your lovely hugs,
Your kiss, your touch, your embrace;
Feelings I sometimes didn't understand;
Those feelings paint pictures of your face.

New feelings are sill wonderfully alive,
Especially on those long, lonely days.
Feelings seem to come in so very handy;
I need them today, tomorrow and always.

BETTER ALREADY

I'm feeling better already
And it's just because you asked.
The pity party is done…it's over.
I've finally put down the flask.

I tried to put some make-up on
And dress up in my high heels,
But nothing seemed to work for me;
That telephone call was the deal.

And then you sent a text as well;
That made a world of difference.
I felt my head starting to clear.
My body strengthened its defence.

Your concern about my well-being,
Has become my security blanket.
For you it seems *au natural;*
I personally 'high rank' it!

ATTACHED

The tremor in your voice touches my soul.
I feel so very connected; easily so whole.
The old was good and the future's bright,
Like a vacation starting off just right.

Conquering the many hills and vales,
Protecting the sparks; that never fails.
Removing the edge, caress you from harm.
Many lingering thoughts, appetizing and warm!

NOW

Feelin'…missin'…yearnin'
Oooh!...creases…petals…lips
My orchid…your antenna
Come!

SIX TWO

At six foot two and one ninety two,
This bronze tower of manhood stands;
Arms with long reach and gentle speech,
Black hairs, now silvery strands.

His work is fishing and feeding and fun
And family and friends are all like one;
Ne'er shy is he of recanting his days,
His children, his loves, his womanizing ways.

But you can't completely blame him;
You're probably wondering why;
With a smile that seems so inviting,
You'll give your all to him and then cry.

He's more innocent than you can imagine
But responds like many men would.
At six foot two and one ninety two,
Stands this bronze tower of manhood.

THA BROTHA

There is no otha
Like you brotha,
Walking, strides like no one can,
A great provider; just a real man.
You smile and laugh and folks do look,
Think you have tha happiness book.
You work hard and you love hard too,
 That's why, that's just why you got the two;
And two more will come if you're not lookin'
And take your heart and send you cookin'.
There is the brotha.
Gotcha on the radar,
'Cause I never watch ya
Man, you live so far,
But how close you stay
With me night and day.
Emails and cell phone
Make a call, write a text.
I patiently wait.
Oh no, I'm not vexed.
Tha Brotha,
Cannot be called by any otha name.
Friday or Saturday or any other day
Only you know your game.
I'll play along;
You know me quite well
And I am ready;
I know you won't tell.
That's tha brotha!

BLISS!

Do you know I really love you?
Do you know that I do care?
Do you feel my heart just yearning,
For you always to be here?

Does it matter that I love you?
Do you ever wonder where
All this magical love comes from,
For you through me, my Dear?

Say, have you ever given any thought
To the time we spend together?
To heartfelt things that we've expressed
Repeatedly to one another?

Or how we hugged and kissed and played
And cooked and cleaned and washed
Then call on Dell to help us out
And count all of our cash?

A sci-fi movie, latest release,
We're on the ball with that;
White screen down, projector on,
Stay up all night and watch.

But Honey, when you're not here with me
Sometimes I cannot sleep.
I do not have the will to go
Into a slumber deep.

Dusting becomes attractive,
Furniture I want to rearrange;
Midnight with glaring music and
I start to make the change.

My neighbours must know for sure
That something has gone awry,
With one set of footsteps over them,
I laugh and sing and cry.

A most appealing smile you have;
Disposition that's unmatched.
As I dust the picture frame I see
That you're a real good catch.

I'm comforted in knowing
How much you truly care.
Telephone calls and emails
Make distance seem so near.

Does it matter that I love you?
Does it matter that I care?
Let my love flow profusely,
Howe'er it will my Dear.

Oh blissful feeling stay with me
For ever and one day.
Inspire me, no matter what,
My love for you to stay.

SINCE THE LAST TIME

Since the last time I saw you
A few changes did take place.
Vague is my recollection
Of your countenance; your face.

Your smile is almost missing
From my memory so deep.
Your touch and warm embrace
Slid somewhere far beneath.

Since the last time that I saw you
Things seem so undefined;
Your love for me seems limited
And shadowy in my mind.

And since that very last time
I visited with your mother.
Unclear it is to me right now
Whether I liked you or your brother.

Since the last time I saw you
I've tried hard to remember,
What we did or just when.
Was it in January or December?

I WANT A MAN

This is a public service announcement brought to you by S.A.M.S. The Society for the Advancement of Mind Shapers. [Spoken in the queen's English]

I want a man! I want a man!
One single, solitary man.
A want a man!
Married, single, widowed divorced, or separated;
I want a man.
A brown or black or white man,
A tall or short man,
A slim or fat man,
I want a man.
A young or old man.
I'm only asking for <u>one.</u>
*One **M.A.N**!*

Ladies and gentlemen, thank you for your attention.

[Sometimes I think that this is what runs through the minds of many young, female professionals, whose biological clocks are <u>quickly ticking</u> away and who are having great difficulty in finding 'Mr. Right'. Sadly and unexpectedly, now many will settle for the mediocre.]

A PRAYER FOR US

"Thank you God for my partner, lover and friend; the one that has been a gift to my life. Thank you God for our respective families and the beautiful relationship we share. God, as we go through this day, we thank you for this privilege. Father up above, thanks, praise and glory to Your name, for having sent your Son Jesus, to die on the cross for the redemption of our sins. Hallelujah for Your greatness, for blessing us with the ability to see, speak, walk and communicate openly with trust to each other and to You. Heavenly Father you know our hearts and our minds and we trust and rest in knowing that You will constantly guard and guide us from evil and harm. Protect us as You always do and surround us with Your everlasting love as we surround each other the same way. Teach us to understand each other, Dear God as we go through the years and appreciate each other for our individuality.

Thank You for the love that You have bestowed upon us for the time that we have spent together thus far. Bless our friends, dear God, and help us all to understand and respect the institution of marriage and its significance. Teach us this day and always, to find the line that will keep our marriage sacred as we continue to praise and thank You for our relationship.

You are the highest and best Teacher and Friend, Dear God, and we love and adore You as we learn more from You. Speak to our hearts and minds so that we can exercise patience, understanding, and care toward one another. Let our commitment be shown with compassion and our love with lasting beauty and an anxiety to please You. Protect us with Your helmet of salvation, shield of faith, breastplate of righteousness and have our feet shod with the preparation of the gospel of peace.

Thanks be to God for all our friends, family and those who come across our lives daily. Help us to recognize good from evil and be able to stand for that which is pleasing to Your desires. Shield us and keep us pure and holy. Thank You Dear God, for the all the wonderful blessings bestowed upon us, and we look to the day that You will pour out the storehouse of blessings that You have promised us as Your children, so that we too may be a blessing to others. We claim the victory and ask these favors in Jesus' name.

Amen."

EMOTION OF REGARD AND AFFECTION

For love reveals so much about me;
It weighs and measures every single mood,
Of every feeling and I disagree.
Already I am full of Cupid's food.
Pray, tell how fortunate I have become
To know truth and love intertwined as one?
No edict keeps these hearts away from home,
But at a canter, is willingly strong.
Stares, looking for the constellation bright.
Cares unravelled for yet another night.
Emotion of regard and affection,
Stay and wrestle; let's see who is the strong;
Or walk away and lose beauty's passion;
Or for generations, stay in fashion.

Section 3)
SENSE OF SPIRITUALITY

A DAY WITHOUT PRAYERS

I did not put my prayers
On today's list of things to do.
My day went totally upside down;
My mind felt that way too.

At work, I had the toughest time.
Clients were all dissatisfied.
They're usually quite easy to please;
Today, I simply cried.

I did not put my prayers
Not even in my head,
Nor whispered 'Thank you' to the Lord.
No word of gratitude said.

I barely avoided an accident,
But couldn't avoid road rage.
Then stuck in traffic for hours;
My car felt like a cage.

I did not put any prayers
In my children's hearts and minds.
Now finally home, it's like a zoo,
Everything was hard to find.

I will never again leave my prayers
Dear god, they mean so much.
You take my cares and all my fears
Just because I was in touch.

DEAR GOD...THANK YOU!

Jennifer P. Lumley

WAITING TO PRAY

While you wait to finally turn eight,
You are now so much closer to ten;
And four year old brother is like no other,
Has a longer wait than you before then.

Now at fifteen, you anticipate sixteen,
Then soon, the age of majority.
Voice starts to change, body's rearranged;
Voting, college and maybe a fraternity.

At age twenty one, the fun's just begun.
You can't wait to be twenty five,
Because when you do, you'll be certain to tell
Your parents that you have ARRIVED!!!

Remember all the time you've waited?
How you paced up and down on the floor?
How you rattled your fingers on the tabletop?
Waiting anxiously for your date at the door?

When all of this time you could have whispered
A prayer to your Saviour and Lord.
Waiting would not have seemed so tough
And you definitely would not be bored.

A prayer for the needy, the homeless and sad,
The aged, the lonely and depressed;
A prayer to make their hearts, once again glad
And put their hearts and minds at rest.

A simple prayer for those at war,
For those soldiers who didn't come home.
A prayer for the family of those
Who rested their loved ones in a tomb.

Prayer for the leadership of our country dear;
For world violence to come to an end.
For teachers and preachers and engineers,
The oppressors, the oppressed and our friends.

So the next time you find yourself waiting
For maybe, let's say, a few years,
Be still; be still, for a moment in life's cycle
And remember someone needs your prayers.

Jennifer P. Lumley

THE MAKER

I look at the stretch of beaches
On the island of Jamaica;
In awe I wonder and declare
The artistic style of the Maker.

The spatial relation of sky and sea,
Creates what is the horizon.
Beyond the mist where they both kiss,
For sun settings and sun risings.

The Maker snugly etched mountains
Indelibly against the skies;
And soft clouds stretch or bundle up,
Shading the sun from my eyes.

Caves are just where they're supposed to be,
Emplaced trees in forests take a stance.
Rivers, streams and brooks keep running;
They'll come this way but once.

Yes, the Maker perfectly appointed
The objects in the constellation;
And naturally, without help from man,
He arranged this configuration.

The Maker organized the animal kingdom;
Ants busy with their chores.
Schools of fish swim in precise order;
You know the Maker was sure.

The depiction in the mirror tells,
That the Maker did something else.
Each lash, each nail, thoughts and glance,
He made for me to cherish.

Fresh air, food, my family and friends
He made provisions for;
Personality, awareness, my caramel skin,
He made for me and more.

Is there any wonder then,
Why I should love Him so much?
Warmth and skills and talents new;
The Maker's wonderful touch.

Quickly each day life passes by;
The Maker has shown us the way.
Love is ours if we only try.
Let that quest begin today!

LET THERE BE LIGHT

Nyctophobia can be lessened or even cured as one goes from childhood to adulthood. Sleep deprivation accompanied by ill-health are sometimes the result of this fear of darkness. The lack of light brings ghastly fear to the minds of many people, adults and children alike. Do we know why? More than sixty per cent of the adults said they did not know, but more than eighty per cent of the children said they knew. They knew, without a doubt, that something terrible was going to happen. They knew with certainty that someone, usually the 'boogyman' would take them away if it were dark. Heaven forbid you to turn off the regular lights, before turning on the night light! Loud shrieks, shrill screams, and hollers would fill the air, until the situation changed. <u>We need light; let there be light</u>.

As early as verse 2 in Genesis 1, the first book of the Bible, we read of the darkness that filled the void. This void was absolute; it was nothing. Soon however, God said *"Let there be light"* and there was light all over. The light of all creation; light that gives life to everything in the universe. In astrophysics and cosmology it is called the BIG BANG THEORY. Call it what you may, I am sincerely grateful that God created man **after** the proclamation of light upon the face of the earth. Man needed light. All things in the universe come as a result of the presence of the light.

Light stimulated man's sense of sight, allowing him to see what God had created and the things over which he had dominion. That physical light was in the sun, the moon and the stars. It was and still is that visible spectrum of electro-magnetic radiation from about 390 to 740 Nano Meter in wave length; that light that travels at approximately 186,285 miles per second. I cannot think, nor do I know of anything that travels as quickly as light. As a matter of FACT, nothing travels faster than light. <u>Light is and has the ultimate speed and velocity</u>.

The human perception of the brightness of light is called the INTENSITY or amplitude. The second dimension of light is its

FREQUENCY. This is what the human eye sees as the color. The third property of light is its POLARIZATION or its angle of vibration, which is not perceptible by human eyes under ordinary circumstances. Man uses light. Let there be light.

Due to the wave-particle duality of matter, light exhibits properties of both waves and particles simultaneously. The question still resounds in the minds of today's scientists, unanswered. What is light? There are continuously new manifestations of light being discovered. The uses and applications are MANIFEST.

There are many words that we associate in our everyday lives with the word *light*. Some include SUN, EDISON, RADIANCE, ILLUMINATION, EMBER, PRISM, BRIGHTNESS, GLOW, CANDLE, BEACON, FIRE and LAMP. Spiritually, we are led by THE LIGHT. Refer to James 1 V7. It tells us that *"Every good gift and every perfect gift is from above, coming down from the Father of lights with whom there is no variation or shadow, due to change."* We want that Light.

Regardless of what else may change, our light will not go dim. Light is a constant of nature AND WITH THIS Light, we can have no spiritual blackout. Our Father does not cause us to stumble over each other or bump into objects, because He is the light and He does not change."Neither do men light a candle, and put it under a bushel, but on a candlestick; and it giveth light unto all that are in the house." Matt: 5:15. When we stumble, it is usually because we have chosen the wrong path, sometimes carelessly, sometimes deliberately or by allowing others to decide for us. When our choices are not right, we often want to hide them in dark places, where there is no light. We do **NOT** want them to be seen. But Matthew 5:16 says *"Let your light so shine before men, that they may see your good works, and glorify your Father which is in heaven."*

When you do the right, you have the privilege of having God's word as *a" lamp to your feet and a light unto your path"* as it is found in Psalm 119v105. It surrounds you. Darkness and night time has a thick density that seems perpetual, but the light from a single, small candle can dispel it and change it to bright clarity. I John Chapter 1 tells us that *"In Him was life and the life was the light of men. The light shines in the darkness and the darkness has not overcome it."* So you begin to realize that no matter how many dark roles there are in life, they flee from our spiritual stage, with just a single gleam of light. Their roles are over.

We are also reminded in John 8v12 that *"I (God) am the light of the world. Whosoever follows me will not walk in darkness but will have the light of life."* Now that is one of the best and most sincere promises, I have ever heard and known. It is the symbol of God Himself. Understand the importance of **THE LIGHT**.

Rainbows and Radar

The rainbow, that visible spectrum of the electro-magnetic radiation, was given as a promise from God after the great flood and it is this important element of light for which we yearn. That Red, Orange, Yellow, Green, Blue, Violet and Indigo arch!!! This beautiful arch of vibrant colors visible in the sky is caused by the refraction and dispersion of the sun's light by water droplets in the atmosphere. Just imagine! Then there are PRISMS that refract light according to their individual wavelengths and produce a beautiful, harmonious rainbow of colours.

Another word associated with light is RADAR, a word coined in 1941 as an acronym for RAdio Detecetion And Ranging. It is the only word used both as an acronym and a palindrome (reads the same backwards as forward, e.g. madam). Radar is how the cop stops you when you are driving too fast on the highway; it is an object detection system that uses electromagnetic waves to identify the range, altitude, direction or speed of both moving and fixed objects, such as motor vehicles, aircraft, weather formations and terrain. These systems must properly overcome unwanted signals in order to focus on the target of interest; in other words the SIGNAL-TO-NOISE-RATIO [SNR] The higher the SNR the better it is in isolating actual targets from the surrounding noise signals AND THE GREATER THE CHANCES OF YOU

GETTING A SPEEEDING TICKET!!! Most times, a wonderful way of saving your life as well as the lives of others.

Light as we know it is also the tri-unity of radiant energy. Similarly, there is the Holy Trinity – the Father, the Son and the Holy Spirit. That is, the Light, the Son of Light and the Holy Spirit. We cannot see light and not know it. Similarly, we cannot confound any part of the Trinity, nor can we divide its substance. Faith is the most basic truth in having salvation and that means believing in the Holy Trinity.
Isaiah 60:1 – *"Arise, shine for your light has come and the glory of the Lord rises upon you"* Man depends on the Light.

Properties and Powers of Light

With light there is HEAT, LIGHT and ACTINISM. The infra-red rays are the warming, life-giving rays, like the love of the Father that is visible to man. Look around you! Plants are growing and all manner of God's love is on display. The ultra-violet rays are the chemical, change-producing rays that are invisible and yet typifies the Spirit's transforming energy. It is not seen although it will start to SHOW in the way we live after that transformation.

Light allows man to stay connected through communication all over the world using Fibre optics. It is a manner of guiding the light through glass fibres, smaller than the width of a human's hair.

God has equipped man with the use of the LASER beams; that is Light through Amplified Stimulted-emmission Electro-magnetic Radiation. This is the method by which light can be harnessed and amplified in one unique length regime so that the most delicate of surgery can be performed even on the eye and yet those same Laser beams can machine or cut through steel! **This is the power of light**...its delicacy and its strength.

Some additional words that we will connect with light will now include: LIFE, AWAKENING, JOY, AWARENESS, REVELATION, LIGHTENING, SPARKLE, PHOTOSYNTHESIS, GROWTH,

REFLECTION, WARMTH, SECURITY, PROTECTION and UNDERSTANDING.

We know also of words such as: radio-waves, micro-waves, x-rays, gamma-rays as well as infra-red rays and blue-rays.

So we now know that light possesses some distinct, maybe even peculiar qualities. It can be **visible and invisible** depending on what part of the wave length you are. Light can be **warm or hot**. Light can be **gentle or powerful**. Light is both **delicate and destructive**. All of these encompass the POWER of light. Light is oh so much more to be discovered. Light is **so simple and yet so complex!**

On what part of the wave length are you? Can you see God and do you know the Light from where you sit or stand? Isn't God just wonderful and to be praised? Only light can penetrate the depth of the universe. Pure light is pure love. Light is the messenger of life.

As people who have come to know the true and ultimate God, let us then:

    Absorb the Light
    Accept the Light
    Awaken to the Light
    Sleep with the Light
    Be comforted by the Light
    Be led by the Light
    Carry the Light
    Emanate the Light
    Hear the Light
    Identify with the Light
    Stay with the Light
    Walk with the Light
    Talk about the Light
    Listen to the Light
    Show the Light
    Understand the Light
    Keep the Light
    Share the Light
    Uphold the Light

Use the Light
Focus on the Light
Follow the Light
Intensify the Light
Lean on the Light
Meditate on the Light
Pursue the Light
Seek the Light
Find the Light
Shine the Light

 Whatever form light takes, man admires it and God wants to provide it, so you do not have to scream, yell or holler to get it. Read the Word, praise and thank God for being the Light and dispel all fears. Keep Him in your heart always and no matter how dark it may **SEEM,** God will always light your way.

Matt 5 v 14-16:
Ye are the light of the world. A city that is set on a hill cannot be hid.
AMEN.

Jesus bids us shine with a clear, pure light,
Like a little candle burning in the night;
In this world of darkness, we must shine,
You in your small corner, and I in mine.
Jesus bids us shine, first of all for Him;
Well He sees and knows it if our light is dim;
He looks down from heaven, sees us shine,
You in your small corner, and I in mine.
Jesus bids us shine, then, for all around,
Many kinds of darkness in this world abound:
Sin, and want, and sorrow-we must shine,
You in your small corner, and I in mine.
Lyrics: Susan Warner
Music: Edwin O. Excell.

Jennifer P. Lumley

"It's better to light one more candle than to rail about the dark." Eleanor Roosevelt.

SEASONS

Bless the Lord oh my soul
And all that is within me.
On a winter's day I'm never cold;
His warmth I always feel.

Then in a sigh the spring time comes;
My soul doth loudly sing:
'It is no secret what God can do'
Colourful flowers He brings.

Summertime living is divine;
Picnics and parties unending.
In a quiet place a prayer goes up
For sunshine, He is sending.

Autumn gently creeps around,
Millions of leaves on the grass;
There is a joy that fills my soul,
Knowing change has come to pass.

Jennifer P. Lumley

THE SPIRIT OF THE DOLLAR

On the back of that dollar you spend each day,
Are the Latin words 'ANNUIT COEPTIS',
Meaning 'God favor our undertakings'
Most people don't even take notice.

Just below you see 'NOVUS ORDO SECLORUM'.
That stands for "A new order of the ages'.
Post-depression; start of a new American era;
Originally from the Eclogue of Virgil's pages.

The compact pyramid of thirteen strata,
To this day remains unfinished.
It represents solidarity, unity and strength;
Glory surrounds the eye in the Zenith.

There are thirteen stars above the eagle's head,
In its talon, a bunch of thirteen arrows;
The same number of stripes is in the flag
When counted, though it seems so narrow.

Transformation, renewal and regeneration,
All associated with the number thirteen.
'ANNUIT COEPTIS' has thirteen letters,
Quite significant on the dollar green.

The beautiful, radiant eye of Providence,
Is neither left or right eye, but Divine;
Its glory extends over the shield and beyond,
Atop the pyramid it does shine.

Reliance on a people of the Divine is designed,
As the eye of Providence in a triangle sits.
'E PLURIBIS UNUM', Out of Many One;
The result of Father, Son and Holy Spirit.

Imagine how many dollars you have spent,
Never paying attention to those details.
Discover more when you're not busy shopping;
Investigate how much more can be unveiled.

IN GOD WE TRUST.

MY LORD'S SACRIFICE

Lord in these times called 'modern days',
We praise your name as we go our ways;
But soon after, if atrocities confront us,
Rather than calling on You, we cuss and fuss.

We fuss about the smallest subjects;
Miniscule things become the greatest objects.
When soft words spoken could've done the job,
Happiness is removed and our joy is robbed.

Dear God I pray You, never to forget,
My cares are yours; no more tears wept.
Humbly I beseech Thee, if it be Your will,
I'll never forget Thee and of You, I'll be filled.

Precious Lord surround me with patience, I pray,
And good will and friendship as I go through each day.
Help me please to remember the sacrifice You made,
With Your life on a cross; although crucified, you stayed.

Amen.

RHYTHM OR MOOD

Who makes the music and my heart skip a beat?
Who makes the butterflies flutter by in the heat?
Who makes the rainbow seem so much brighter?
It's the rhythm of the heart and the mood of the writer.

How come the hummingbird can easily fly backwards?
How elegant it seems and for others it's so awkward.
How magnificent its plumage whenever he sights her;
It's the rhythm of the heart and the mood of the writer.

When volcanoes erupt and spew out molten rock;
When an English girl is dressed up in her pretty frock;
When the challenge is up to show that you're a fighter;
You find the rhythm of the heart and the mood of the writer.

 But where does the rhythm of the heart come from?
And the *mood of the writer*, is that some new song?
The rhythm is created from your connection with the Lord
And the mood is steadfast love given by God.

SHARING GOD'S GIFTS

Imagine all God's wonderful gifts;

Multiply those thoughts, then share them.

Amplify your praises to the Creator;

Garner the energy in your system;

Intensify your spiritual fortitude,

Novel though this act may appear;

Exemplify the Creator's love on earth,

Driven by His loving kindness and care.

THE LOVE OF THE CREATOR IS SO PERFECT, IT IS ALMOST IMPOSSIBLE TO IMAGINE. NONETHELESS, HE IS FAITHFUL TO HIS PROMISE. IT IS REAL.

Let us hold fast to the profession of our faith without wavering... Hebrews 10:23

KNOWING WHEN TO BE SILENT

You can conquer many, just by keeping a quiet hush,
Many also are healed without words, but with a simple touch.
Silence inherently provides, a posture for holy worship;
Freedom from noise and distraction; no movement of the lip.

Silence is that thing that signifies, respect for self and others;
A fresh renewal for wonder at the world and love for one another.
It's not necessarily keeping secrets or being anti-social.
It takes strength and a conditioned mind, not always to be vocal.

It is environmentally safe, and strongly recommended.
An indication of submission to God, for your soul to be amended.
Reverence shown, since silence is a condition of tranquility;
It is the stage that provides for, effective, spiritual sensitivity.

Silence when temptation's near and pulling on your tongue;
Silence sometimes when you do right and others do you wrong.
Silence to help show children how to communicate without speech;
Silence used to build character; a new level of confidence to reach.

And if you ever have to speak, be impeccable with your silver word;
Speaking should reflect what you mean; do not gossip or be absurd.
The power of your word should contain, truth, love and an awareness;
A projection of your own reality, with integrity and fairness.

You can conquer many, just by keeping a quiet hush,
Many also are healed without words, but with a simple touch.
The art of being silent is a science, and an admirable art;
Speech is silver; silence is golden; an inspiration from the heart.

SO, GOD...

(A conversation with God)

So God, what were You thinking when You created me?
That You'd have someone to praise You, and I'd live in victory?
What could have really come over You, to have made me...a sinner?
Think You would have won my soul and then get invited to a dinner?
And what would we have talked about, as we sat down and dined?
How You'd give Your one and only Son? That I would not have repined?

Tell me something else dear Father God, why is it so very difficult,
To live the life You want for me? My failed attempt seems an insult.
Some days I just don't even bother. It's too hard to live like You.
Though I am made in Your image, Your likeness does not shine through.
Don't You understand me yet dear God? Why do You keep on trying?
Am I so valuable to You? Is that now why You are crying?

Oh God I don't want You to cry, and let the whole world see.
I promise You a better life. I promise, better living for me.
I cannot continually let You down, after all the sacrifices You've made.
With little effort I know I can. I won't let my talents die or fade.
I have to be a good example, 'cause God people see and they watch;
And through my daily example, some other lives You will touch.

So why God, did You create me? To be an economic dependent,
On family or state and not be a butterfly in a field just splendent?
Why have I so long suffered, with illnesses that won't leave my bone?
My name has neither fame nor fortune, and my heart isn't made from stone.
I wake up every single day, praising Your holy name the very same,
For I am in my rightful mind; I can see, feel and move. I'm not lame.

Life can be so unpleasant God, and turbulent stress puts me ill at ease.
The strength of character I've developed, I'll use to make You pleased.
When those monthly bills are hard to pay and temptation says 'Give in',
Your spirit says 'Simply lean on my strong arm, for together we will win'.
I must say I admire You God, as You sit on Your throne high above.
I know now why You created me and You're such an easy God to love.

Section 4)
OUR UNIVERSE

TODAY

Dewdrops barely perched upon the trees all around;
Humming birds in their beauty, never touch the ground.
New rosebuds poke their heads up to the bright, beautiful sky;
And butterflies come grace the earth as they flutter by.

The cool summer breeze drifts by and it just gently awakens
Tiny insects on the ground and the leaves on plants are shaken.
Bees afloat in the air, seem like they are suspended;
Their honey-making day shift starts, work is far from ended.

Clouds shift away and make a place for the sun to show its face;
The sun sheds warmth upon the earth, bringing forth its grace.
A new today has come again and time gently unfolds,
Pregnant with opportunities for all the willing souls.

HAIKU

Haiku (pronounced High-koo) is a popular, traditional form of Japanese poetry. It is usually structured with 17 syllables in 3 line verses. The first and third lines contain 5 syllables each and the middle line contains 7 syllables. Traditionally, haikus describe nature.

[1]
Mother earth's floor shifts
Large scale tremors in one country
Reconnects the world.

[2]
White snow unending
Flakes all in differing shapes
Snow birds come singing.

[3]
Windy morning bright
Cheering leaves on bent branches
Nature's language heard.

[4]
Sun rays separate clouds
Footprints traced on sandy beach
Rippling waves foam.

RISE NUBIA, RISE

From south to north flows the river Nile
Through ancient Nubia, my home;
Africa's earliest Black civilization,
Where exotic animals still roam.

The natural wealth and fertile farms,
Offered ebony, ivory and stability;
An ethnic group lived in a culture rich,
Sharing in a unified dynasty.

See the pottery with geometric designs,
How many stories do they tell?
The constantly burning incense
Carries a beautifully rich smell.

Africa's ancient, north-eastern region,
South of Egypt, north of the Sudan,
Had the best mines near the river Nile,
Lake Nasser now swallows most of its land.

Nubia, you gave all for my ancestors and me,
But now you have chosen to sink.
Your history will have to be rewritten,
Without the decadence; without the stink.

Dear Nubia, how they've abused you;
We suffered pharaonic iconography.
Throughout history we've stood our ground,
While suffering the slave trade atrocities.

Dearest Nubia, home once ago and now,
We've paid dearly the highest price;
But with faith and dreams of a resilient people.
Once again, yes I know, Nubia will rise!

ROBBERY OF A CONTINENT

Waves from the sea
Brought unto me
The news of my ancestors;
How they travelled all jammed
Snatched and in a small hole crammed,
When they left the continent;
Wide open space, and life content.

Rivers told my soul
They'd all been bold
But they all didn't survive.
Only a few were still alive;
Respect for their lives disappeared,
When forced from the continent;
With wide open space and life content.

The new minority,
Having no seniority.
Twenty two percent of the world's land;
Of earth's continent, it runs second.
Living in tenement held by so-called superior.
Ripped from the continent;
Where they had wide open space to their content.

Tacit winds of ill omen,
Mourn the death of our men;
A people in thrall of men spewed from afar.
Generations at dis-ease; a permanent scar;
Gems robbed and sold for no profit to us,
When they raped the continent;
Leaving wide open space to their own content.

Life started in Motherland,
Love started with the African.
The lines of the Sahara quite distinct;
Beautiful Kilimanjaro, in indelible ink.
African Diaspora robbed of its dignity.
Grabbed; nay torn from the continent,
Leaving wide open space and life in discontent!

God gave us His son, so our lives would be won;
Not lost at sea, but our souls would be free
If we claimed the victory,
Through the principles of:
1. Umoja = Unity;
2. Kujichagulia =Self-determination;
3. Ujima = Collective work and Responsibility;
4. Ujamaa = Cooperative Economics;
5. Nia = Purpose;
6. Kuumba = Creativity; and
7. Imani = Faith.

Faith to believe in all our hearts, in our people, our parents, our teachers, our leaders and the righteousness and victory of our struggle!

Both Hathor on the left and Bat on the right flank Menkaure in this fourth Dynasty triad statue, the goddesses are providing the authority for him to be king; note the feather of Ma'at held by the emblem on Bat's crown - *Cairo Museum*

MOON CHEERS

Here's to the moon and all that it offers,
Cheers to the moonbeams causing lots of laughter.
Cheers to the hunk of cheese shining so bright;
And cheers to the planet that lights up the night.

Here's to the moon, I'll raise my glass gain,
Cheers to the moon, with a smile almost vain.
Cheers to that moon, earthlings want to discover;
Its temperature, its taste, its fragrance its texture.

Here's to the moon showing half of its face;
Fishermen work with you, all in good grace.
Cheers to the moon, in its first quarter;
Sometime making the night seem so much shorter.

Here's to the moon, farmers stick to the schedule;
Cheers to the moon, that unreachable tool.
Cheers to the moon at planting and reaping;
Bright, beautiful moon, do you ever go sleeping?

Here' to the moon, that makes a silvery sea.
Cheers to the moon that smiles down at me;
Cheers to the moon, making mercury lakes;
Cheers to the moon, rivers slither like snakes.

Here's to the moon, from all four directions,
Cheers to the moon and the whole constellation.
Cheers to the moon, of you I never tire;
Lots of cheers here and there, that's what I desire.

Jennifer P. Lumley

WHO CAME WITH COLUMBUS?

Each of us that went to school
Studied the history of Columbus;
And we were able to pass history tests
But all this time, the joke was on us.

HIS STORY that Isabel and Ferdinand heard
About his voyages on all these three ships,
Made them so pleased with 'New World' DISCOVERY,
That they commissioned him on additional trips.

DISCOVER: means that you are the first,
First to find and to make known.
It doesn't mean total disregard for truth;
Here the seed of the propensity to lie gets sown.

Hear this: they said one man came with three ships.
Strange? True? We believe what they told us.
Pinta, Nina, Santa Maria, but who else?
Might sound simple, but it's utterly ridiculous!

So who else came with Columbus?
Seriously, were there any friends?
So what were the names of the other two men
Who manned the ship? Or were they women?

What was their role in all of this?
How come no other names were called?
I wonder if it were two Black men;
Well trained, and strong and tall?

I've always thought it's worth some consideration.
No longer should our children be disrespected;
Why give them all these lies to swallow,
Leaving them totally unprotected.

Native Indians in the Caribbean,
Plied the oceans between neighboring islands,
While fishing and securing their meals for families,
Then relaxing on the paradise, white sands.

No more Columbus day celebration for me;
See if you can find out who came with him.
I'm very keen and interested in my HISTORY.
Please tell me, **who came with him?**

Jennifer P. Lumley

NO NAME HURRICANE

Simple, gentle, swaying moves,
Noticeable on the elegant evergreen
Are promptly redefined in direction,
When harsh winds blow unseen.

A smile appears upon my face,
As the evergreen dips and sways.
Every branch and limb begins to move;
My senses are simply amazed.

I'm tickled pink at the stories conveyed,
As it swerves and displays its charm,
In its elite, entertaining, ballroom dance;
The cool beat of the waltz gets warm.

The winds whirled hard and picked up speed
Causing continual, leviathan sounds
And beat the high buildings undeservingly,
Whooshing through the trees all around.

The raindrops joined in and spattered heavily
As though ten were joined in one
And when the wind got wind of that,
It scattered the branches across the lawn.

The wind resounded like a marching band;
Painfully loud and uncomfortably close,
With a perpetual promise to return,
To make the foundation of the earth loose.

The womb of the cloud broke forth its waters;
Heaven's powers are no longer concealed.
Every dark, dry, place got darker and wet;
The hurricane without a name was revealed.

Section 5)
SHORT STORIES

BUTTERFLY FRIENDSHIP

So there you are, now thinking to yourself that you could be in love and that love could be in you; but why? She brought your mind to a higher level of acceptable thinking and you even dare to philosophize, in your anguish. Should she be a friend…only? She is the butterfly you wanted to just rest on a flower or as much as touch a leaf, so you could catch her and bottle her for as long or as short as you wished and then release on your own whim, if you desired; damn well knowing that she would never be the same vibrant person you met.

You could have watched from a distance too. But oh no. You chose to catch the butterfly and something happened to have caused you to want to let go. Too late. You are filled with her light heartedness and her fresh new outlook on life; yet you wonder how she could be packaged with such a great deal of intellect. No one really cared to have shared with you on the level that she did. She now flies around incessantly in your head day and night; more vigorously, vivaciously and more beautifully than ever. And you cannot pull yourself away.

New long term thinking is in place. You dare to go further, for as long as you can. She's resting on your shoulder without being a nuisance. She decorates your life. You are in love and love is in you. Friends <u>only</u>, you said?

JAMAICAN HIGH SCHOOL GIRLS
[From the eyes of a high school boy]

How perfectly pressed were the pleats in her tunic, even after a full day at school. Jamaican high school girls had something about them that sometimes could not be identified; something sweet and innocent. Maybe it was a combination of natural qualities such as their body shape, skin tone and sheer elegance that captivated the aesthetic senses. How come boys did not see that in a girl in primary school? Boys...yes boys were too busy playing cricket or rounders and sometimes hitting a girl and dashing off, outrunning her, simply because he could. Now here in high school, girls are viewed differently. They could be seen walking two abreast quietly talking and smiling...about what? You can't really hear but a boy is especially pleased to get the two for one deal; see two girls at one glance. Wow! Who could ask for anything more?

Dust free shoes in Jamaica! Who ever heard of that? All the girls were like that though and they never stared at the boys. How could that be? Maybe they did not like boys or dusty shoes or beads of sweat, or the smell of their bodies after a good, long game of soccer; but boys had to play at least one sport and enjoyed the sticky feel of wetness under their armpits. Girls were noticeably different even though they would come to watch the boys in competition or at matches.

The sweet purity of a Jamaican school girl seemed to have poured out even more and was far more noticeable, when I attended my friend's sixteenth birthday party, under his parents' guide, at their home. We were all within the sixteen age range and these girls in party dresses were suddenly...women. We looked good but boy oh boy, they were charming! After talking, laughing and eating, the slow music played and there was a kind of hush that came over the room. The people dancing suddenly departed from the dance floor and like the red sea, it parted in two; girls on one side of the room and boys on the other.

I got brave and asked a girl for her company to reopen the dance floor. Seemed like a pretty simple act, right? No! My palms sweated and my heart was pounding out of my chest. I thought of the idea of her possibly saying no to me, and how devastating and so embarrassing it would have been, but she saved me with a kind, soft "Yes, ok". Or did she? Then why am I feeling like I was in an arena and a bull or a lion would come out to attack me, while I was totally unarmed? Why all of these wrong, discontented feelings? I also realized that I was being cheered on by the fellows, for having reopened the dance floor. Cheers suddenly sounded like "boos" and they were loud, long an unending. It felt like three million years before another couple finally came to the dance floor and rescued me from all the cheering. Their entry to the small, living room dance floor was not as grand and certainly not as embarrassing.

My partner's mode of dress was simply elegant. It allowed you to see just enough curvatures on her beautiful body but covered enough for active imagination to take place. The soft, tender smile on her countenance, hinted at her happiness and her grace. Her Afro hairdo was so perfect, glistening from the light that shone from the DJ's table. She smelt of baby powder behind her ears and a light perfume from the lotion she used, surrounded her entire body. She seemed to be following my lead with soft stepping movements and was confident. Her skin was ebony with a rich, healthy glow in her cheeks. I had seen the muscle tone in her arms and her chiseled calves. She was a goddess. I needed to do nothing but try to understand and experience the beauty of all of Africa in this one creature. It brought me to my Blackness; my own beauty and my obligation to respect her as the Mother of all eternity.

Jennifer P. Lumley

LETTER TO AFRIKA

Dearest Mama,

I hope you are keeping well. I am finally ready for the bar exams, after all. As I walk through the streets of my community, I cannot help but reflect upon and recognize the value of the education I am getting, not just in law school, but in adjusting to the new environment with the weather, values system and attitudes being so different from home. Mama, you have made great sacrifices and I'm sure if my father were alive, he would appreciate you even more for it.

Some days I wonder if African women, as we know them, will ever again, have their well deserved legal rights and status restored. I see women that are in despair and DISREPAIR; lonely, underprivileged, disenfranchised and burdened with cares they cannot possibly handle. They face the challenge of rearing children on their own, because the fathers have disappeared, have died or have been imprisoned. Some get caught up in unnecessary conflicts with other women over the few remaining men that barely add up to mediocrity. Many of our African women are illiterate and have been manipulated then isolated by the system of law that is in place here. I see that their self-esteem is shattered, but not lost. So I continue to believe in Imani – my FAITH that I will never lose.

Mama, I am anxious to get through this bar exam so that I can earn a living of my own and start being of service to the African women I have mentioned. They need an advocate to assist and educate them on the ravages that human trafficking plays on the lives of African families; an advocate to assist in readjusting their thoughts, hopes and dreams, so that they can be catapulted into an improved socio-economic status in a dignified manner. African women are courageous, strong and hungry for the support and opportunity, to again walk with strides of confidence, like I do, Mama. I'm hopeful that with the appropriate shift in gears of legal rights, there will be the promotion of justice and equality, so that women will have children by choice and not by accident; that they can raise children that are socially wholesome, productive and focused; that their communities will maximize the quality of life through educated parents, teachers and caregivers. Pretty soon we will have more women and children, leading healthier, extended lives because of change I dream will take place expeditiously; change that will cause enlightenment and an awakening of self.

Imagine these women with a deep sense of purpose, empowered to rise to their intellectual potential, paying keen attention to their role in society; never being satisfied until they see the result of their determination to be extraordinary in their achievements. I can visualize the entrepreneur, the nurse, the doctor, the CEO and the engineer peering out of the eyes of these women, in whom I dare to believe. I can hear them speaking impeccably and with integrity; holding their own in political offices and being an example for generations to come. Mama, you know that being economically self reliant is an important aspect of African life and I continue to believe in KUUMBA; that spirit of cooperative economics that I learned at home. It is imperative that more women like me, get together with the same mind set and work toward this common goal; that of "**promoting strength and community through culture and information**".

I have great appreciation, love and respect for you, Mama Africa.

With love,

Jamaica.

---

*   African Women's Alliance.

AND NOW HE'S NINETY!

Mosi-oa-Tunya Falls, better known as Victoria Falls in Zambia, is one of the world's seven natural wonders. It is beautiful, awesome and spectacular. The natives call it "The smoke that thunders." Now picture a man, a Jamaican man, playing the role of husband, father, grandfather, uncle, cousin, friend, brother, confidante; working as a builder and contractor. Picture a man migrating with his family to the United States of America in 1968. What a bold move! What a cold move! He left behind the lush greenery, white, sandy beaches, thundering rainy nights, beautiful, blue skies, and the heat of the bright sunny days. He also left the sweet star apple, a variety of succulent mangoes, juice dripping down your hand, sweet sop, healthy sour sop, seedy nesberries, juicy coco plum, june plum, guava, water coconut and jack fruit. Here is a man in pursuit of financial betterment for his family. Here is a man who has reaped the fruit of his labour. He was a pioneer in his time. He was spectacular.

If perchance you are at a special vantage point in life, to have seen him in action, you would certainly understand the parallel being drawn between Victoria Falls and this stalwart, whose boundless enthusiasm and careful determination enabled him as a sage and a visionary to have made such a move. He knows so much, he stayed in touch; he has nurtured and cared, and cooked so everyone would be fed. If you were not at that special vantage point, however, you can only try to imagine how awesome this man has been and continues to be, based on this description. He is Jamaican!

Make no mistake, he does go home; YES, H.O.M.E. to Jamaica, as often as he can, but he has made this place his new place of abode and his children are happy. So too, are the friends, and spouses of his children, who do not have a *POPS* of their own. So Pops has an extended family and those of us that know all his children, including my husband and me, always have an opening line to our conversations: that is "HOW IS POPS?" Pops we love and respect you dearly!

Let us raise a toast to Pops on this, his 90th birthday and to the legacy with which God has entrusted upon him thus far: his children, grand children, great grand children and a host of friends and family.

The Old man, Pop, Poppy and Pa,
Today we honor and praise this man;
He's always to be remembered,
Not only on this his 90th birthday,
But from January to December.
So here's to this fine man and all you do;
You are truly loved and appreciated.
This year it's not a kiss and a tie
And "Hey Pops, or just a "hi";
This year it's "I'm glad we're related"

Here's to more happy and healthy years ahead!!!

DEPTH OF DARKNESS

He watched her almost staring, losing track of the time and ignoring the usual conversation with his regular Friday night buddies at the sports bar. She entered alone, and he could see her sparkling eyes even though she held her head low. She appeared to be single, but normally in an establishment like this, singles usually come in groups or were accompanied by some man, spouse, fiancé, boyfriend or 'wanna-be-something' in her life. Who said she was single anyway? She wore her clothes like an angel and was bejeweled with nothing authentic; nothing genuine, just real cheap and fake. In Jason's eyes, no one wore fake as elegantly as this babe. She was really hot. Jason's interpretation of her presence was HEAVENLY!

"Is this finally my lucky day?" he thought. "Is this the girl of my dreams?" She was mesmeric. He watched intently from across the room as she ordered her drink and could hear her every word as she ordered, but heard nothing his buddies said. Only when his bouncer friend, Ox, stood like a wall in front of his face, did he recognize that his mind was elsewhere. He snapped back into the buddy conversation, missing much of the laughter and the last subjects they'd talked about while he was in his daze. "Someday one of them girl's gonna get you." his friend calmly advised.

He finally made up his mind to approach her, since she did not seem to have a man or girlfriends coming to meet her, so he walked over and said hi. She outrightly rejected him. She was not interested.

A few nights later he saw her again at the same bar, except this time he was alone. "Hello" he said to her nervously. She smiled back and his eyes lit up with anticipation. She did not remember him and completely dumped the conversation he wanted to have. She was not interested and it was clear, but after some pleading she gave him a number.

He called the number many times over the next three months and left his numbers. No response. Never once did she reply. He believed with all his heart, this should be his girl. His feelings were very strong, almost instinctive, so he couldn't give up. He remembered her so clearly, as if it were only yesterday. He knew her well.

Suddenly one day he got a call from her. It was from a pay phone. Why? He wondered, but the invitation to meet was irresistible. She introduced herself and informed him that her cell phone battery had died so she used the public phone. That's settled that. They met at a bar and then had dinner which she turned into a night of passionate love. She was the sweetest girl he had ever met. He was amazed but satisfied; He woke up, she was nowhere, disappeared without a trace. He was no longer intrigued and felt his manhood had been compromised; the conquest was over but he was the victim. She was under his skin plain and simple but gone…that's life.

Just another girl he thought, lucky break on my side. But he could not get her out of his head. She was too amazing. The profile did not fit. He called and called and called, nothing. She did not come to the club, she was gone. An internet trace, that should do it. Bingo! He found her workplace. Account manager at a bank downtown. He turned up there but no one knew of her. This was strange.

He thought that a new club might brighten his spirits and erase her from his thoughts so he turned up at "Club Mango" the new hot spot in town. As he entered he was stopped in his tracks. There she was in the middle of some suits and smiling away. Without a second thought he stormed over and held her hand. She withdrew and asked, "Do I know you?"

"Who is this?" one of the suits asked. "I really don't know" she replied innocently. "Get outa here buddy" the other suit demanded. He realized that he did not even know her name so he retreated with hurt in his eyes. He waited that night sitting in the club, in the dark, not a word, drink after drink, until he saw her leaving with the suits and as they exited the club he approached her again.

"It's a set up" one the suits shouted and suddenly all guns were drawn and pointed at him. His stomach felt hollow and all he could say is "I really love her" Suddenly the place was lit like a stadium and an authoritative voice over the megaphone shouted "Don't move you are all under arrest. There were police and handcuffs everywhere. This was the end he thought. Caught in a major crime bust over a girl he didn't even know.

Suddenly, out of the lights, walked an angel, "This one's OK" she smiled. "He's mine". "Omigosh" He thought. "Is that you?"

"You almost blew my cover" she scolded. "That was stupid. Don't try to find me; I will find you." She chided as she turned and disappeared.

"What's your na. . . .?" he shouted, but she was gone. This is going to be a rough one.

THE AMOUNT OF TIME
I DO NOT HAVE

I really can't begin to tell, 'cause I simply don't have time today,
I truly must get to that second job, so I can get that second pay.
I have the checks that I've been paid, but didn't get to the bank,
The amount of time I did not have, has me driving on an empty tank.
I can hardly stop to fill up now, 'tho I expect bumper to bumper traffic;
Neither can I afford to break down, but I have no time for a mechanic.
I really do not have the time to rest; do you have some time to spare?
I cannot lie down in the bed to sleep; no, maybe I'll just sit in the chair.

I need to reply to Mom's phone calls, she has been so very persistent;
It's Christmas now and I'm so busy; she may just have to wait till Lent.
I haven't had time for proper meals; I'm just grabbing things on the go,
Now I'm having dizzy spells, but I don't have time to let my doctor know.
I do not have much time at all, or many friends; I think it is so unfair:
Yesterday came to such an abrupt end, looks like the same today, I fear.
That deep voice in my house, made me realize that my boy is now a man.
He'd graduated college and is now ready to wed a truly beautiful woman.

He is a man and no longer the little boy for whom I once had no time;
I didn't have time to advise him, so I'm now writing this little rhyme.
Please be forewarned that we all get the same amount of time each day;
It's entirely up to you right now to spend it, in a most rewarding way.
Be thankful and make your days fruitful, make them be of some worth;
Every single tick on the clock takes some energy and some effort.
First be kindest to yourself and then follow up being kind to others;
Think not of the time you do not have; what you DO have is what matters.

Jennifer P. Lumley

A GREETING TO SOLDIERS ON POPPY SUNDAY

Soldiers, Ex-Soldiers, other members of the Executive, members of the clergy, elected officials, distinguished ladies and gentlemen, a pleasant good morning to you.

Today I am honored to be here, in a place of worship. I will return to worship with you because I see that you are children of God and there is spiritual warmth in here. Please make it a point of your duty to worship with me in my home town whenever the spirit moves you – you are always welcome. Consider it your second church home.

It is with sincere gratitude and a deep sense of humility and pride that I have accepted the invitation on behalf of my association, to bring greetings to you on this Poppy Sunday, Remembrance Day, Armistice Day or Veterans' Day. Regardless of what we call it, thank God for our soldiers. As president of my Association, I am fully aware of the magnitude of the office and I will do my utmost to discharge of my duties with credit to those who have confidence in me and to myself.

I bring you greetings from a group of women who have worked hard to live up to the standards set by those who preceded us, the teachers that were tough on us, our parents' expectations of us, but mostly by the high standards that we privately set for ourselves. Once you entered the gates of this most noble institution, you were automatically transformed. You were now marching to the beat of the school's drum; your uniform was different, your rank and serial numbers were assigned to you and as confusing and as frustrating as it seemed, hardly wanting to wait for our five years to end after GCE, when it actually happened we all were at a loss. Were we going to do youth service, apply for work, travel, get married to some fine soldier boy, or move on to University? I was chicken; I opted for an additional 2 years in school so I could clear my head. I said I was doing "A" Levels. I, like many others, could not really believe this fan fare, this razzmatazz, tennis match, netball playing, boy talking, beach going thing would ever end – it did.

Today I thank God for all I got at my high school, I am able to stand before you like a true soldier and march to the beat of any drum and sing songs of praise and read poetry, and prose. You see, like you, I too was in an army. While in high school, I discovered the Girl Guide Association. So now I greet you again, this time wearing the hat of the Worldwide Girl Guide Association that helped me to develop leadership and life skills through challenges and adventures. With ten million girls in one hundred forty five countries, we speak in one voice with our motto "BE PREPARED."

The words of Cecil Spring-Rice must also be familiar to you:
"I vow to thee my country, all earthly things above,
Entire and whole and perfect, the service of my love
The love that asks no questions, the love that stands the tests
That lays upon the altar the dearest and the best
And there's another country, I've heard of long ago
Most dear to them that love her, most great to them that know
We may not count her armies, we may not see her King
Her fortress is a faithful heart, her pride is suffering
And soul by soul and silently her shining bounds increase
And her ways are ways of gentleness, and all her paths are peace."

When written, the song depicted the loyalties that soldiers must have to both their homeland and their heavenly kingdom. Soldiers fought bravely and died valiantly and as we celebrate those courageous men and women with the red poppies that represented the profuse bloodshed of World Wars, let us also remember the white poppies that were introduced as a "desire for peaceful alternatives to military action."

We thank and praise the men and women at war for us right now. I also want to thank all the bold men and women that were ready, willing and able to serve and are now ex-soldiers. Mr. President, as you lead this new army, in an effort to help all ex-soldiers, I implore you to continue this symbiotic relationship with my Association, for we are more alike than different. We join you in the memory that you celebrate today and applaud you in all future endeavors.

The words of Thucydides, the Greek historian, may provide some useful insight. He says that:
"A private man, however successful in his own dealing, if his country perish, is involved in her destruction, but if he be an unprosperous citizen of a prosperous city, he is much more likely to recover. Seeing, then that states can bear the misfortune of individuals, but individuals cannot bear the misfortune of states, let us all stand by our country."

Our President-Elect Barack Obama very graciously and eloquently said in his victory speech about Senator John McCain, and I quote, "He fought long and hard in this campaign, and he fought even longer and harder for the country he loves. He has endured sacrifices for America that most of us cannot begin to imagine and we are better off for the service rendered by this by this brave and selfless leader"

On this solemn day, let me leave you with these words by Lt Col. John McRae. It is one of the most popular poems written after he witnessed the death of his friend:
In Flanders fields the poppies blow
Between the crosses, row on row,
That mark our place; and in the sky
The larks, still bravely singing, fly
Scarce heard amid the guns below.
We are the dead. Short days ago
We lived, felt dawn, saw sunset glow,
Loved, and were loved, and now we lie
In Flanders fields.
Take up our quarrel with the foe:
To you from failing hands we throw
The torch; be yours to hold it high.
If ye break faith with us who die
We shall not sleep, though poppies grow
In Flanders fields.

Ladies and gentlemen, may God ever bless you. Thank you.

Girl Guides

Section 6)
PATOIS

A SO MI SEH

Wen mi done talk, a so mi seh,
A dat mi mean, a so mi seh;
If baby cute, a so mi seh,
Yu nuh like wah mi seh, yuh cyan go weh.

Wen mi done speak, a so mi seh,
Di queen's English, a so mi seh;
American stylee, a so mi seh,
Jamaican patois, srtickly, a deh mi deh.

Mi a yaad man, a so mi seh,
Mi a bad man, a so mi seh.
Mind yuh bizniz, a so mi seh,
Lef di caanaz, just move streggay.

I know good life, a so mi seh.
Because a strife, look weh mi deh.
I soon release, a so mi seh;
Ten years behind bars too lang fi mi stay.

Dance to the beat, a so me seh;
Rock on your feet, a so mi seh;
Don't hang in the street, a so mi seh;
If yuh cyaan tek di heat and di rey rey.

Mi a yessiday bad man, a so mi seh,
And today's deportee, fi dem sen go weh.
When mi done talk, a so mi seh,
A dat mi mean and a so mi seh.

TODAY'S MANIKIN

Oonu look inna department store
An see statue a maggle fashion?
Skirt and blouse and shaats and more;
Life-size dummy wid a passion.

Is nat a aadnerry ooman dummy;
Look pon dem fram head to toe.
Pickney wudda call dem 'Mummy'
If yuh nuh 'urry an tell dem 'no.'

Firs' time manikin used to wite,
Wid slenda face an' pink cheek;
An' likkle nose an' small baddy,
An' elegant figga fi look sleek.

But nowadays yuh go a store
An look good inna di glass,
Di manikin look back pan yuh,
Like seh yuh mussi deh faas.

Some ave nice, allive calla skin,
An some daak an velvet smood;
Wid nose-hole lakka funnow gate
An talk 'bout <u>AT-TI-TUDE</u>!!!

Missis all kinky hair deh wear
Ball head an' braids an lacks,
An batty cack aff eena jeans;
Ongle a Black ooman ave dat!

A tell yuh, we really mek some strides,
'Cause dem want di clothes fi sell;
Suh Black an white dummy deh pon display,
Wid a resonant message fi instill.

Jennifer P. Lumley

ENOUGH DUPPY

Mi have enough a duppy now
Frah well before mi bawn,
An me decide fi cum a wul,
One day well before dawn.

A dat time dem seh rolling calf
Busy a walk pan street;
An wooden foot man de pon a hurry,
Fi go see if im cyan get real feet.

Convert ooman dem jus a come home
Frah singing all nite lang,
Dung a nine nite weh Maas Tam dead;
Mussy sing out every sang.

Di neighbor wah live nex door a we,
Fi har husband as well jus done dead.
An nutt'n but black clothes she nuh wear,
Even di wrap wa de pon her head.

Di big ol gate weh outta front,
Have wah big hellevva red claat;
Fi keep out ooman duppy weh madman kill;
She wen pretty and cute and shaat.

So now mi staat fi go a church,
See a man wid him hass and cyaat.
Him dress di haas wid ribban and flowaz,
Now him ongle lef fi gi' it a bath.

Yuh cyaan look pon di has too lang
Cause di man carry a whip,
An him wi run yuh dung an beat yuh
From yuh shoulder to yuh hip.

Yuh know di man name Takkumah heart
Di same one, 'Ice-inna-soup'?
Mi hear seh him a black art man;
Him nyam chap-up pickney inna group.

Den like a spite mi go ah private school,
A private school dem seh;
Wid nuns fi teach we di lessons,
An duppy fi frighten wi weh.

Cause di blasted school deh right next to
One graveyaad divided by a fence.
Di sweetest mango dem hang ova de grave
Fi duppy nyam dem; dat mek sense?

Any day one drap affa di tree
Mi bet yuh nah go fah; seh feh
Yuh wlling fi place a bet wid me
But mi nah go ova deh

Yuh cyaan pint inna graveyaad neida,
Or else yuh finga wi ratten aff;
Yuh affi spit pan it an put 'i backa yuh,
Duppy mussi deh watch an laugh.

Last week on mi way home from school,
People gyadda suh mi tink a fyah.
Mi bore chu di crowd fi go look and see,
Mi buck up pon di BLACK MORIAH!!!

Mi suh frighten, mi run come home
Because now mi go see duppy,
An hear strange sounds andaneat mi bed,
But it was mi pretty likkle puppy!

POPPY'S 90TH BIRTHDAY TRIBUTE

A nuff ooman de wanda
How fi raise pickney lakka yuh;
How fi plait hair and cook food
An smile wen yuh dun wah yuh do.

A nuff ooman wah married
To yuh son dem far an near,
Affi fall in line an duh wha right,
Or else jus' live in fear.

'Cause Poppy house always full a food;
Hungry belly nah tek dem.
So Poppy live whole heap more years,
Dis is a toas' fram family an fren.

SEAMAN KHAKI

Is a new work mi get last week,
Mi cyaant even stop fi drink mi tea;
And mi almost get up late today:
Mi haffi go press mi seaman khaki.

It nuh easy to be a Security yuh nuh,
Yuh haffi always look criss and clean;
'Cause some people will jus walk pass yuh,
Like dem doan know what you mean.

Yuh fi see mi seaman khaki shirt and pants,
Seam dem tan up staach an well press;
All of sudden mi full a cold sweat,
An a shootin' pain run crass mi chess.

Mi staat move forward fi lean pan a chair,
Ask if di pain nuh waan lean wid mi.
So mi shiff di right foot fi go siddung,
Di pain tan up an seh 'Wi a go see'.

Wen mi open mi mout fi call mi fren,
A feel like Excalibah inna mi choat;
Mi yeye dem full a wata now,
Mi soun lakka half ded 'ol goat.

Mi cyaan siddung, mi cyaan tan up,
Mi cyaan move 'roun, mi cyaan talk;
Mi cyaan call fi help, mi cyaan halla,
Mi cyan ongle wish mi cudda walk.

Jennifer P. Lumley

It feel like mi stuck deh fi two day straight,
In fact more like two an a half;
But ah determine seh ah nah dead tannup.
A gwine get help fran di 'aaspital staff.

To dis day a cyaan begin fi tell yuh
How I kech a di emergency room,
Fully clad inna blue aaspital gown,
Mi glad mi neh inna mi tomb.

Two dacta come fi duh examination;
Mi feel betta fi see more dan one;
Right dere pan spat mi wi' able fi get
An opinion an' a determination.

Di shaat one seh im tink mi have gas,
Di tall one him seh 'Oh no'
'Gas doesn't manifest itself like this'.
Now di two a dem staat to talk low.

Den shaaty an langy lala come togadda,
Mi tink dem aggo sen mi a mi yaad;
Dem gang up pan mi an tell mi seh
Dem affi sen mi go a di psych ward.

Now mi well vex an well waan run way
Go see my private dacta inna town
An lef di two mad man dem right deh
But mi still have on di blue gown.

Mi just quietly and sadly excuse misself,
Seh now mi haffi use di ress room
A head straight fi di ooman toilet
Weh ah put aan ooman clothes and went ZOOOM!

A run lef mi shiny boots an socks,
Amost losing mi pride an dignity.
I willing fi sacrifice all a dat
But ah cyaaan lef mi seaman khaki.

Ah realize fi di first time inna mi life
Dat mawnin a nevva drink no tea;
An gas nevva mek fenny fi tek me up,
While mi bizzy de press seaman khaki.

So nuh matta how important di matta;
Even if is a job fi do security;
Nuh stress too much 'bout seaman khaki.
Kechup yuh stomach wid likkle hat tea.

Jennifer P. Lumley

THE APPLE OF MY 'I'

I man always feel comfortable
And irie wid **I** man self;
And Jah know **I** pray only to Jah
Fi **I** food, **I** health and **I** strength.
I forward from **I** pad recently
Go inna wan store go browse;
I tek wan look and look again
I man curiosity was aroused.

I see a ting dem call *iphone*
I tink is **I** language dem adopt.
I see on a shelf pon di odda side
An *ipod nano* well wrapped.
So **I** man start to ask some question;
Di store clerk look young an green,
Like di ilalloo fresh from di gyade'n,
Wah good fi **I** liver an **I** spleen.

But **I** man really was ipressed
I appreci-love it, but si yah'
Him tell **I** 'bout *ipod touch screen*
And di portable media player.
I man hear di details an' overstan
ipod shuffle, ipod classic, ipod hi-fi
Him IQ high, talk 'bout *ipod connector*
Ipod earphones and *itunes* fi **I** and **I**

Only Jah coulda mek nuff people
Embrace di term **'I'** widdout a fight.
Dem irie wid I man language now
It gawn high tech and outta sight.
I man mek sure seh di **I** buy,
One *ipod* fi **I** sista and **I** queen.
Di most newly unveiled *ipad,*
Is fi **I** empress iyah, seen?

MONTEGONIAN GIRL

A Montego Bay mi come from
And a Montego Bay mi mean.
'The Friendly Republic', The 'Second City'
'The Tourist Capital', aiya, seen?

And yuh dare fi call mi country girl;
Yuh need a lesson inna geography.
All mi see a town a mad people an' mawga dawg;
Look like destitution and catastrophe.

Sunday dinna fi oonuh a some likkle sprat.
Inna Montego Bay dat use fi bait.
Who a nuh pick packet a run a racket
An a gwaan like say dem a look date.

Is not like mi cum yah fi tear yuh dung,
Because yuh bawn aanda clack;
Oonu mussi did need a medical visa,
Or maybe di aaspital wen lack.

Mi nevva carry waata pon mi head
And have pig and cow fi go feed,
Or plant baddu and dig up yam,
Anyway a how yuh wudda eat?

Many days I stroll from home to the beach
With not an earthly care in the world;
Special rays of bright sun shines on me,
Because I'm a Montegonian girl.

The stretch of white sand patiently waits
Till ah slip off mi sandals an' shorts;
And the waves welcome me with ripples
Like the pulse of the ocean's heart.

Sea grapes become readily available
And provide me with that quick snack;
The almond trees all congregate
Making a shade for my face and back.

I am tanned and thin; a Montegonian
You can see it; tell the truth!
Strands of hair are golden brown
And bronze down to the root.

So when you come to Montego Bay
A willing fi show yuh aroun',
Wid a friendly Republican welcome,
Like a true Montegonian, proud.

SWEET, SWEET JAMAICA

Some pretty-pretty basket wid nice tings
An some ooman wid nuff-nuff sweety,
Used to siddung in front a school gate,
Ah sell gizzada, drops an rock candy.

Di oomam dem lap dem shiff an' dem skirt,
An' dem siddung pon a stool or a stump,
Apron pocket a ovaflow wid pickney money:
Dem nah lose a penny inna gyabage dump.

Bus-mi-jaw, Stagga back, Bustamante backbone:
A wan sweety dat wid all tree name.
Grater cake, peanut brittle, juju, motorcar;
Back and front have dem owna claim to fame.

Yuh memba wen rock steady come inna style
An reggae sweety staat to keep im owna beat?
Mi did still love mi icy mint an ginga lag,
Hasham, tambrin ball, toto and tie teet.

Dem mek wan likkle flat , pink ching gum,
A boomerang da wan deh did name;
Some used to have a comic strip fi wrapper,
Oddas had sum different kine a game.

Some time yuh buy hay-penny wut a pone,
Taste like it sweeten wid honey.
Or ching gum inna silva or gole file,
Wah look like real-real money.

Police button, stretch candy, jackass caan,
Hacks, plantain tart an mint ball,
Chinese sweety, bazooka joe and taffee,
Paradise plum was the best of all.

Sweet-sweet ice cream cake an icicle,
Fudge, roas' peanut an animal crackaz;
Cigarette sweety one whola-whola pack,
Plus brawta if yuh have good mannaz.

A likkle man wid a cyaat an some surrup,
Stan up ova suh, anda di shade all alone.
Him full up nuff cup wid some shave ice,
An a bawl out 'Snow cone, snow cone!

Summa com, school dun; yuh haffi get a washout;
So yuh go spen time wid granny a country;
She give yuh castor oil, herb, senna an salts;
But afta all, it weh well-well wutti!

Jennifer P. Lumley

A STILL LIFE

How very wandaful it is fi know
Seh mi go a school an pay attention
To maths an science ca dem important
But wah me always love is **the elocution.**

Clear, distinct, expressive speech,
On Litany or concise articulation,
Mix wid a drap a Spanish or French
Or German fi extraordinary execution.

So if mi shoulda go a any restarant
Y mi quiero mi cake *a la mode*
Dem betta serve it up *pronto*
Cause a nuh like mi a talk inna code.

Den wen mi tell mi fren *bon apetit,*
It nuh mean 'bun up yuh teet', oh dear!
Warsaw Concierto discussion end up,
As' walk sharp and shelta'; *au contraire.*

How shallow is education these days;
I just wonder, *'muss es sien'.*
Muchas gracias todos mis profesores;
Mi *duckuno* was *muy bien.*

Dis a nuh artificial intelligence; it real
Pon a global melting pot ever changing
Wi need fi know more dan wan language dese days,
As the world keeps rearranging.

Ces't la vie, los ninos will be ok
Don't worry, *no te preocupe;*
The spirit of the times, the *Zeitgeist*
And teachers, *simper sint in flore.*

Sayonara and Adios, dat mean mi gawn;
*Meda w'asé and Danke mean m*i thank you
Mis noches sin ti mean mi lonely a night time,
A still life doah mi fren...*adieu.*

[Alphabetical order of Languages included: Asante, (Ghana) English, French, German, Italian, Jamaican, Japanese, Latin, Polish, Spanish, Twi.(Ghana)]

MARRIS

Tall an' serious, black an' trang,
  Neat grey beard pon a grey hair man,
    Chess inna di air lakka Baaba Milla pijin;
      Wen 'im walk pass di gal dem, head a spin.
        Edumication, trent an' confidence, him nuh lack,
        All man shudda seek dat, both white an' black;
          But yuh haffi persistent an' try fi achieve.
            Like mi fren Marris; him nuh tap believe.
          Mar, Mar mi seh; Maurice, they say;
            Your company has a leader dere to stay.
            This earth has been blessed regally,
              Wid a man of your stature; legally…**Jamaican!!!**

CHO RHAATID

Blurdeeks, any ah oonu si dat?
Kiss mi neck, a suh 'i fat!
Blouse and skirt, it come again;
Mi ayzbell, set good mi fren.
Cackroach, it sounn' like **dandymite**
Falleetee, mi nah stay ya tinnite.
Blow wow, now rain staat to fall
Royal caad, dis wi mek big man bawl.
But si yah, nuh even badda tease,
To neck back, now **yuh fennay grease!**
Coase joke, a di ongle ting yuh cyan chat.
Shugga plum, soun much betta dan dat.
Rackstone ! Look lke fight a go pap;
Nuh get **buff inna fi yuh blouse cup.**
Jeeezam peezam, a how 'im suh lie?
Rhaaco lily caad, mi haffi sigh.
An' him **soak up** sometime yuh si!
Jackass tail root, him nuh fren fi mi.
Blurdipeps bwoy, dissa sitt'n bitta;
Bax front man, look pan di litta!.
Him **chap im ten;** one irie dread.
She comfortable, **gawn to bed.**
Cho rhaatid man; why di strife?
Anyway A STILL LIFE.

Jamaican Idioms: The use of words, sounds and accents, characteristic of
a specific group of people.

MI IS A VERB

Mi is a VERB, mi is an action word,
Expressing existence and occurrence in the world;
Mi is a VERB, mi is an action word,
Representing the state of being in this world.

In a sentence, an essential part of the predicate,
Asserting something about di subject.
Go is a verb, like when you go to the market;
In a sentence dat's how complete it get.

CHORUS: *Mi is a VERB, mi is an action word,*
Expressing existence and occurrence in the world;
Mi is a VERB, mi is an action word,
Representing the state of being in this world.

To lead a healthy life is a really good ting;
To join in dis sang, mean seh yuh want to sing;
To crown him wid yuh haat, gwine make him king;
To marry mean say yuh have a partner an a ring.

CHORUS: *Mi is a VERB, mi is an action word,*
Expressing existence and occurrence in the world;
Mi is a VERB, mi is an action word,
Representing the state of being in this world.

Mi is a mover and shaker; not an excuse-maker;
Mi is a mover and shaker; not an order-taker;
Love is a verb, it is an action word,
Expressing existence and occurrence in the world.

Love is a verb, it is a state of mind;
Love mek yuh happy and it also mek yuh kind;
A phenomenon big, the only ties that bind;
Love is what make everything just fine.

Love is a VERB, love is an action word,
Expressing existence and occurrence in the world;
Mi is a VERB, mi is an action word,
Representing the state of being in this world.
Love is a VERB, love is an action word,
Love is a VERB, love is an action word,
Love is a VERB, love is an action word,
Love is a VERB.

TWEETY LUMLEY

Tidday, tidday, mi ah tell yuh seh,
Mi tannup inna di showa,
An memba mi likkle blue parakeet;
Har vim, har vigga an har powa.

She used to tek har likkle beak,
Fi open up di cage,
An fly out an frighten people weh nuh know;
An get dem inna rage.

She used to hear di waata run
Soon a mawnin time inna di bath;
She bruk outta cage, straight a bathroom,
A deh suh fi har fun staat.

Di heap a moisture weh cum up from
Di waata wah run dung,
Get har excited and quite pleased;
Fedda cack up an ready fi fun.

Wen mi eat cold cereal a mawnin time
An a try hurry fi go a work,
Fram spoon touch plate, das all she hear
Mek she gi her cage door a jerk.

She siddung pon di side a mi bowl
An pick-up pick-up some can flakes,
Den wen dat dun she slide right dung
Inna di milk an staat to bathe.

Yuh could'n even bex wid her
She was so sweet an pretty
Yuh just fix a different bowl fi yusself
And lef dat one fi Miss Tweety.

Den when mi staat to hand wash dishes,
An di pipe waata staat to run,
She hurry up fly out come perch pon mi shoulda
An chirp some pretty likkle sang.

I tell yuh, mi blue parakeet truly brought
Songs of mirth into my life;
And laughter and sincere happiness;
Tweety Lumley was a real delight!

Jennifer P. Lumley

TIFF TONE DEAD

Ello. Ello. Ell..O. Please? I cannat ear yuh prappa.
Please? Mek a walk go outside yah suh. A mighta ear yuh betta.
Ello. Def ayz gi lawya chubble.
O Mavis yuh. Mi tink a weh smaddy. Eeehy, ello.
Seh wah? Yuh tek a fence to dat?
Mi a yuh, mi woudda tek 'ouse an' lan tuh. Hey hey.
Yuh cyaan tek joke inna dem yah haad time missis, mi sarry fi yuh.
Repeat…ello. Seh wah? Gaage? Shaat Gaage?
Yuh too lie, tappy. Wen?
Friday? But tidday a Satday! Mi jus see'im Thursday.
Gaage? Ded? How ee fi ded? Him cyaan ded.
Aat attack? Dat mean **'im ded!**
A chu sump'n, Mavis, ar a joke yuh deh mek?
Seh dem fine 'im wid veAga?
Den 'im **tiff dead!**
Wha??? An two young gal?
Nat wan? Two?
But laaawks, shaat Gaage mus **tiff, tone, ded!**
Ello…ello Mavis yu yearin' mi Mavis?
Mavis, how yuh have summuch details an suh soon too?
Das right, mi fegget seh Gaage weh like you.
But mi nevva know she yuh tek interes inna Gaage.
So a it mek yuh so sensitive an de tek offence.
Ush mi dear. A nevva mean to be 'fearancing
In mattaz dat duzz'n cancern mi.
Ello, ello please. Dem yah now-a-daze phone yuh see.
Now Mavis get discanneck. Mek I get back to mi day's work.
She betta dan mi, ca him mus lef sump'n inna him will fi 'ar.
Some people cyan just lucky, eee? If a egg Mavis inna di red.
Dem seh *lucky bawn betta dan well bred.*
Now shi really get 'ouse an' land fi chu.
A cyaan hardly cum to misself, doah.
Gaage tiff, tone, dead; Mavis rich; but a **STILL LIFE.**

MI GLAD TOO QUICK

A get a pretty, juicy mango,
Wah feel nice and look fit and firm;
A wash it and leggo a big bite,
Ongle fi find seh it have in worm.

A run go a di post office because
A get registered mail;
A happy fi feel important so till;
Di letta seh mi fren inna jail.

A get free ticket fi go a jazz fest,
Mi glad; mi put it safe inna mi jacket.
Mi reach di gate wid a big smile,
But by den smaddy pick i outta mi packet.

So mi go a di gym fi go see if me
Couldda work aaff some a di stress;
Nuh do nutt'n more dan get excessive
And tear up di muscles inna mi chess!

Mi reach mi yaad ready fi go bathe,
Afta a long hard day's wuk,
Ongle fi see seh di waata gawn;
Mi simply outta luck.

Later mi bathe and spray up wid cologne;
Cack up eena bed like sweet bwoy Rick;
Mi wife cum eena bed wid attitude, vex;
Look like each time, mi glad too quick!

UPON BEING FIFTY

Mi fren say him want a copy
Of mi newly published book fi buy.
Mi ring di bell an him open di door;
Him puddung wan big-big sigh.

Him tell me say how im proud a mi,
But wanda wah tek mi so long;
Him expect me fi publish book already,
And even staat write some sang.

Den him ask, outta curiosity him say,
How old mi is right now.
Mi laugh, cause him retired and old;
Mi say "fifty" and tek a bow.

Di two a wi bus outta laugh
'Cause him really nuh dat old;
Him say mi look good fi mi age, an
Some a him fren dat age look like ol fowl.

Mi blush likkle bit an den tank him
Fi di truck load of compliment.
Him pay fi di book; mi still a smile;
Mi feel like sixteen: sweet and innocent.

Mi fren say him "Madda function well,
At one hundred year ole"; an a chu man.
Him remind mi say "More stride lef fi mek"
"Cause at fifty, you a ongle half a ooman!"

EPITOME OF A LADY

Lawd missis, yuh hat so till
Yuh exquisite an' always inna style;
Look like say yuh own Landan bridge;
Yuh drive all di man dem wild.

Yuh step wid confidence an class;
Yuh skin pretty an yuh nuh haffi show aff;
Grace, elegance, finesse and etiquette;
A mussi yuh name di Golden Calf.

Mi hear say di Leaning Tower of Piza
Straighten up when yuh de near;
An dat di Eiffel Tower light up bright,
Fi see dis beautiful creature, rare.

Di mountain shake an sea rebel,
Volcanic eruption tek place;
Yuh calla pawn di hearts of great-great kings,
All fighting to seek your embrace.

Yuh have di grace of a fashion model;
Polished, poised an easy wid yuh sride;
Yuh countenance pleasant but businesslike,
As across the floor you glide.

And yuh love yuh darling husband,
Because him cherish yuh like a treasure;
An oonu a one anadda best fren;
Fi know people like yuh is a pleasure!

LEN A DAY

Mi gran faada have a ten acre trech a lan
An mi memba when I was a bwoy of ten,
Him prepare fi go plant up di whole prapatty;
Di neighba dem know dem have a day fi len.

Grampa stack up all him tool an such,
Him pipe kotch pon di side a him mout;
And di lady dem pack up di food fi go cook;
Bwoy pickney cyaan wait fi hunt bud; no doubt.

Of course yuh know say yuh ten acre a lan
Nuh inna di vicinity a yuh house;
Yuh haffi mek enough time fi traipse go deh
An still feel energetic an aroused.

Because yu haffi walk up an dung gully,
Di man dem chop some walking stick,
Fi mek it easier fi walk over sink hole
An jus betta fi negotiate di whole trip.

Wen yuh reach, a space clear right away,
So nuff big cooking can tek place;
An di delegated ooman dem set up tings,
Because dem nuh have nuh time fi waste.

Mi granny she nuh carry matches go a bush.
She so cunning an so smart, she nuh stap;
She mek sure all bases covered,
She carry fire all di way inna dry coc'nat.

Now yuh know yuh haffi find di spring,
Because yuh need wata fi cook;
An yuh know say bamboo point to wata,
So a deh so yuh haffi go look.

Di man dem fork and rake an dig and plant
And mek rows up and dung di prapatty.
No time fi waste, ongle sweat a bus;
Dem wuk an sing; dem nuh cackatty.

Anadda haad day's work is done;
People eat an staat mek back dem way,
To dem various yaad , till smaddy else need
Di district fi help dem, an come **len a day**.

Penny nuh come outta mi grampa packet.
Len a day is practice from Africa.
Being economically self reliant is important,
Das why we used to **len a day** a Jamaica.

We nevva go a bank go borrow money,
Fi go get tractor and tractor driva.
We is a smaat thinkimg set of people;
Jamaicans is a group of survivah.

If only dem wouldda jus continue,
Wid **len a day** and practices such as dese,
J A would'n inna suh much financial chubble;
We wouldda deh sail wid ease.

Let this be a charge to all Jamaicans and people of Jamaican heritage worldwide, to be resolute in finding a way to 'len a day' to help rebuild the Jamaican paradise we once called home. Things look bleak, but can get better. Let us all help to save it from the weight of the financial burden and the general state of maelstrom in which it struggles.

Jennifer P. Lumley

A WHO COME WID COLUMBUS

Di whole a we wah go a school,
Study history 'bout Columbus;
An we able fi pass di history test,
But all dis time, di joke was on us.

HIS STORY wah Isabel and Ferdinand hear,
'Bout him voyage on all dese tree ships;
Dem so pleased wid 'New World'DISCOVERY,
Dat dem commission him back pon more trips.

DISCOVER: mean say dat yuh a di first,
First to find an to mek known.
It nuh mean total disregard fi truth;
Here di the seed of the propensity to lie get sown.

Hear dis: dem say wan man come wid tree ship.
Strange? True? We believe wah dem tell us.
Pinta, Nina, Santa Maria, but who else?
Might sound simple, but it is utterly ridiculous!

So a who else come wid Columbus?
Mi nuh mean di tree ship dem.
A wah di adda two man name,
Who manned the ship? Or were they women?

What was fi dem role in all a dis?
How come no adda name nuh call?
A wanda if it was two Black men;
Well trained an strong an tall?

I tink it's wort some consideration
No longer should di children be disrespected
Whammeck we gi' dem dese lies fi swallow,
Leaving dem totally unprotected.

Native Indians in the Caribbean,
Plied the oceans between neighboring islands,
While fishing and securing their families' meals,
Dhen relaxing on the paradise, white sands.

Nuh more Columbus day celebration fi me;
See if yuh can find out a who come wid him.
Mi very much interested inna mi true HISTORY.
Tell mi nuh please, **a who come wid him?**

TWO DIFFRANT CALLA BOOT

'Oonu move outta mi pass right now.
Cyar an chuck stap right deh suh.
Mi haffi ketch di five fifty one train.
No ramp wid mi; a wuk mi a go'.

Di train hat an crowded an nat wan seat,
Except ova we di mad man siddung.
Wi rack an lean pon wan anadda,
An move wen madeeks lang out him tongue.

'Quick, quick lady, jus please cyan move;
Tek di wheelchair outta mi way.'
A wan an a half hour mi travel already
Mi cyaan late fi wuk tidday.

Mi hustle, jay walk mi watch stap light,
Yes, yes mi ketch di shuttle to mi destination;
Mi caffee nearly spill right a di elevatah door;
It staat to look like total frustration.

Alright, two hours a mi day jus gawn;
Mi successful; ah mek it to mi affice door.
Mi almos go cack up mi foot pan mi desk;
Is a good ting mi look dung pan di floor.

A two diffrant calla boot mi have aan;
A dat happen when yu get dress inna daak.
Den summuch people see me a hurry,
An nat even wan a dem wudda talk!

Well evenchwally mi coworker dem see;
An wi laugh lang an talk hard 'bout it.
Wi all agree say we behaving like lemmings,
Since we come to dis country; we admit.

Fi di fuss time we suddung quite seriously,
Talking 'bout the time we spen commuting;
An calculated di four hours each day,
Dats twenty hours a week- no disputing.

Dats half of a forty hour work week,
Moving back an forth fi earn wages;
Den di cost involved in dis constant trek,
Crossword puzzle book wid whole heap a pages.

Imagine if I cudda get dat time fi vacation,
All nine hundred and sixty hours fi di year;
Or get paid straight, or betta, time an a half;
Wid mi dressing, mi wudda tek more care.

Calculate dem howaz ova a twenty year period;
A wudda dun retire lang-lang time.
Ah nineteen thousand two hundred howaz dat;
Truss me a wudda do it at the drap of a dime.

In dis economy, mi glad fi know mi have a job,
No money worries, thank God, no complaints.
Mi mind haffi jus ready fi dis eveling commute,
Ketch a nap or do mi crossword puzzle again.

MAD-ESTRIAN

Yuh cudda tan deh peep-peep, pawp-pawp so till,
Mi nah ansa because mi a nuh cyaar;
An furda more mi cyan mek out yuh face.
Bad mannaz! Plus yuh deh too far.

It wudda serve yuh betta fi come likkle closa,
And maybe if mi see di licence plate,
Mi cudda know if yuh a mi faada firs' cousin
From town, aldoah it still kinda late.

Mi say nuh peep-peep affa mi again.
Mi nuh have nuh haan fi toot yuh back.
Mek a walk aff an lef yuh alone,
Before yuh splash gutta waata pon mi pretty frack.

Yuh finally mek up yuh mind fi pass,
But yuh still haffi tun yuh head and look.
Real genkleman doan display behavia lakka dat;
It say so inna di 'Etiquette to Pedestrian' book.

Peep-peep, toot-toot, beep-beep, pawp-pawp
Whole day is all yuh cyan hear
When yuh walk from airport to downtown
As a pedestrian, yuh walk in fear.

'OL GINAL

Ginalship wi help yuh only sometime,
Bloodsucker, but ongle fi so lang,
'Cause wen it all come to di light, hootipeck
Yuh haffi go sing a whole new sang.

Yuh bandoolu people outta money,
Like a tricksta yuh tek weh deh lan.
Doublecrassa, yuh transfer dem cyar;
Dem a walk an yuh a drive inna fashan.

People jewelry a nuh nutt'n fi yuh flash
An wear like say a yuh own.
Yuh deh wid smaddy smaddy now;
Guineanag, careful of dose seeds sown.

Bandit blood run chu yuh pretenda vein;
Tricksta, das why yuh live inna big house,
But yuh parasite personality wi nevva change;
Snake inna grass; bunchy fowl louse.

Hussla, con artist, scoundrel, scamp
Yuh story nuh really add up to nutt'n.
Leech life an permanent borrowing
Lead to exploitation; you is a glutton.

Criticism nuh mean a ting to yuh ol sponge
Samfie man, skyanka, "transfer" minister;
Yuh evil and vile and wicked; plain tief.
Yuh is a menace an yuh behavior is sinister.

GITTUP, CUM OUT AND GAWN

[An Easter Poem]

What a wicked set a brute dem,
Pontius Pilate and di whole crowd,
Wah mek Jesas walk so far wid a crass,
An dem tan up an mack Him loud-loud.

Dem arres di man fi nutt'n at all,
Him naked except fi a crown o' thawn,
Dem beat an spit pon dear Christ Jesus;
Is lakka say a yessiday Him bawn.

Once dem lead Him off to Calvary
Also known as the "Place of Skull",
More punishment staat to tek place,
Before di place fall inna lull.

Him six hour sufferin' start from di third hour,
Inna three language dem cuss Him "Jewish King";
A three man crucify pon dat deh one single day
An three Mary tan up an' watch Him.

Wan a di Mary was di wife of Clopas,
The odda was Mary Magdalene,
Di third was Him owna loving madda dear,
Dat wipe Him bloody farrid clean-clean.

Dem give Him sour vinegar fi drink,
Wen Him say Him have a thirst.
Well anything cyaan wicked suh?
But it get even far worse.

Him call upon Him faada Gad,
And utta seven diffrant statement;
Di las one say "Dear Faada,
Into yuh han I commit mi spirit".

Yuh know wah really badda mi?
Is when dem pierce Him inna Him side.
God one an ongle pickney bwoy,
Just hung and bled and died!!!

Imagine, now dem tek Him dead body,
Put inna linen burial cloth wid myrrh,
Wid wan big rackstone in front a di tomb,
An three Roman guard fi watch in case Him stir.

Well fi mi Jesas nuh stir dat deh nite,
Him wait suh till when three day done;
Him ascend up into di high Heaven,
Siddung next to God like a good Son.

Di same three Mary dem is who
Was the eyewitnesses to see and know.
Say Jesas tomb was empty now,
And joy staat to ovaflow.

Dem run an go tell di disciple dem,
Say up from di grave He arose.
Aldoagh dem shack dem still celebrate,
It's a mighty triumph o'er His foes.

So tidday, tidday mek wi celebrate,
Fi know say di Messiah atone all a wi sin;
An if Pilate or Herod wen fi try fi wi case
Unlike Jesas we wudda lose; we cudd'n win!

[Sing: Up from the grave He arose, with a mighty triumph o'er His foes]

"*Up from the grave He arose;*
with a mighty triumph o'er His foes;
He arose a victor from the dark domain,
and He lives forever, with his saints to reign.
He arose! He arose! Hallelujah! Christ arose!"

Text and Music by Robert Lowry

Section 7)
JAMAICAN DOUBLE WORDS

JAMAICAN DOUBLE WORDS

Jamaicans have a particular way of making sure that there is total clarity and no ambiguity in their expression about the way they feel, be it good or bad. It is by using any word twice, back to back. So rather than saying something was very good, we say it was 'good good' and if you are wearing a floral print dress it could either be 'pretty pretty' or have 'nuff flowaz flowaz'. Listed below are some of the more commonly used double words by the Jamaican Diaspora.

Try and see how many you've heard or can remember!

(Usually used for emphasis)

Back-back
Bad-bad
Badda-badda
Batta-batta
Bawly-bawly
Bax-bax
Beggy-beggy
Brap-brap
Bruk up-bruk up
Bufu-bufu
Bun-bun
Cass-cass
Chakka-chakka
Chamba-chamba
Chatty-chatty
Chi-chi
Chip up-chip-up
Chu-chu
Cold-cold
Cratch-up-Cratch-up
Crucrumcrum
Cry-cry
Culu-culu

Cunumunu
Curu-curu
Cut eye-cut eye
Deggay-deggay
Different-different
Dugu-dugu
Dutty-dutty
Fassy-fassy
Fenkey-fenkey
Fingle-fingle
Flowaz-flowaz
Fool-fool
Fooley-fooley
Fraidy-fraidy
Fretty-fretty
Funny-funny
Fussy-fussy
Good-good
Goody-goody
Hair up- hair up
Hairy-hairy
Heapa-heapa
Hat-hat (hot-hot)

Haughty-haughty
High-high
Jucky-jucky
Ju-ju
Jus-jus
Kiss up- kiss up
Laughy-laughy
Licky-licky
Low-low
Lucky-lucky
Mawga-mawga
Mash up-mash up
Mouly-mouly
Nasty-nasty
Natty-natty
Nyenge-nyenge
Ningy-ningy
Nevva-nevva
Nice-nice
Nizey-nizey
Nyami-nyami
Nuff-nuff
One-one

Passa-passa
Pewney-pewney
Picky-picky
Pretty-pretty
Pyah-pyah
Red-red
Ripe-ripe
Saaka-saaka
Seedy-seedy
Shiney-shiney
Slubbo-slubbo
Smiley-smiley
Soso-so
Speaky-spokey
Spotty-spotty
Swaaty-swaaty
Sweaty-sweaty
Sweet-sweet
Tear up- tear up
Wagga-wagga
Walky-walky
Washy-washy
Wholey-wholey